To Paul
For the best boss I've
ever had. Thank you,

False Witness

Barbara
Rader

False Witness

Melvin Rader

With a New Afterword by Leonard W. Schroeter

University of Washington Press

Seattle and London

To my sons and daughters
David, Cary, Barbara, Miriam, and Gordon

This 1998 edition of *False Witness*
is part of the All Powers Project,
a multidisciplinary effort
by the University of Washington
to commemorate the 50th anniversary
of the Canwell Committee hearings.

Copyright © 1969, 1979 by the University of Washington Press
Afterword by Leonard W. Schroeter © 1998 by the University of
    Washington Press
Printed in the United States of America

Library of Congress Cataloging-in-Publication Data is available from
the Library of Congress.
ISBN 0-295-97702-7

The paper used in this publication meets the minimum requirements
of American National Standard for Information Sciences—Perma-
nence of Paper for Printed Library Materials, ANSI Z39.48–1984. ∞

If a false witness rise up against any man to testify against him that which is wrong; then both the men between whom the controversy is shall stand before the Lord, before the priests and the judges, which shall be in those days; and the judges shall make diligent inquisition; and behold, if the witness be a false witness, and hath testified falsely against his brother; then shall ye do unto him, as he had thought to have done unto his brother: so shalt thou put the evil away from among you.

DEUTERONOMY

Contents

Introduction

to the

1979 Edition

IN THE years that have elapsed since *False Witness* was first published I have found no reason to change my mind. No one has challenged the accuracy of the narrative, or denied the importance of the issues at stake. The events I narrated, including the fateful hearing before the Washington State Un-American Activities (Canwell) Committee, can now be recognized as foreshadowing the abuses of the McCarthy and Watergate eras—the tossing about of wild charges, the break-in and search, the resort to perjury, the concealment and destruction of evidence, the violation of constitutional rights on grounds of "national security."

During the years before and after the hearing, I was struggling to make clear to myself and my students the nature of human rights. These rights were being violated with unparalleled ferocity during the 1930s and World War II. The deepest depression in history deprived countless human beings of the material means to freedom. Revolutionary movements of great scope and fury scorned the axioms of American democracy. Like many others I was tormented by the clash between two conceptions of freedom—on the one hand a bill of immunities, on the other hand a schedule of claims.

I mean by "immunities" what Madison called "the great rights of mankind"—the rights that were evolved in centuries of political struggle in England and its colonies and embodied in the American Bill of Rights. Freedom is therein conceived as the immunity of individuals and groups from the overweening power of army and police and the arbitrary action of legislators, administrators, and judges. The rights stated in the Bill, at first binding only upon the federal government, have with few exceptions been extended to the states through the Fourteenth Amendment and Supreme Court decisions. These rights include free speech, free assembly, free and independent worship, fair trial, security against unreasonable searches and seizures, due process, and equal protection of the laws. It would be difficult to exaggerate their importance. They are indispensable to the life of a free people.

Nevertheless they are not the entire gamut of human rights. No man is free if he is unable to "pursue happiness"—if he is insecure, hungry, diseased, ignorant, the victim of hate and prejudice. Rights imply not only *being allowed* but *being able*. They include not only the absence of external restraints, but the presence of resources and opportunities to realize one's potentialities and effectuate one's choices. The latter enabling rights I call a schedule of claims, because they require supportive action of government and other social agencies. I also call them "social rights" to distinguish them from the more personal immunities.

The Great Depression underlined their importance. So

far as previous policy had emphasized only immunities, it had left men and women "free" but without the material basis of life. Free human beings must be able to satisfy their fundamental needs, such as the need for food, shelter, clothing, health, education, employment, security, and opportunity. An adequate agenda of freedom must combine the two sets of rights, the immunities and the claims. Widespread recognition of this fact is the enduring legacy of the Depression. My own development as traced in *False Witness* was a deepening appreciation of both kinds of rights. This development was not without doubts, mistakes, tensions, and crises. It is the "inner side" of my narrative.

Although individual and social rights are complementary, they are often pitted against each other in the violent conflicts between extreme individualists and extreme collectivists. The goal of humankind—to come into the plenitude of its being and powers—demands not the clash but the reconciliation of social and individual rights. The individual rights have been frequently violated even in our democracy, as in the Canwell Committee hearings, the McCarthy persecutions, the Watergate scandals, and the many abuses that continue to this day. The social rights also fall vastly short of fulfillment among the poor of all races and nations. Receiving too much to die on but not enough to live on, they exist in a nether-nether land between life and death.

The Washington State Legislature in creating the Canwell Committee may have thought that they were defending individual rights against "un-American activities." In fact the committee was as violative of the bill of immunities as it was intolerant of the schedule of claims. The plain fact is that individual and social rights are inseparable—neither can flourish alone.

[xi]

Consider, for example, freedom of speech. As the Office of War Information declared during World War II, free speech requires far more than the legal right to speak. "The first condition is that the individual have something to say. Literacy is a prerequisite of free speech, and gives it point. Denied education, denied information, suppressed or enslaved, people grow sluggish; their opinions are hardly worth the high privilege of release. Similarly, those who live in terror or in destitution, even though no specific control is placed upon their speech, are as good as gagged. Another condition necessary for free speech is that the people have access to the means of uttering it—to newspapers, to the radio, the public forum. When power or capital is concentrated, when the press is too closely the property of narrow interests, then freedom suffers." Free speech requires a firm social fabric to support it. This is true of all the other individual rights.

Social rights are just as incapable of standing alone. Rosa Luxemburg, the intrepid German socialist murdered by the Nazis, grasped this truth. "Freedom for supporters of the government only, for members of one party only," she declared, "is no freedom at all. Freedom is always freedom for the man who thinks differently. This contention does not spring from a fanatical love of abstract 'justice,' but from the fact that everything which is enlightening, healthy and purifying in political freedom derives from its independent character, and from the fact that freedom loses all its virtue when it becomes a privilege. . . . Without general elections, freedom of the press, freedom of assembly, and freedom of speech, life in every public institution slows down, becomes a caricature of itself, and bureaucracy rises as the only deciding factor. No one can escape the workings of this law." Rosa Luxemburg was a good Marxist who saw more keenly than Lenin the meaning of history.

My gradual realization of the interdependence of individual "immunities" and social "claims" kept me from joining the Communist Party although I was strongly urged to do so. This realization equally restrained me from joining the Right Wing. Others, just as well intentioned, swung to one or the other extreme. The outraged Right attacked the socialists and the outraged Left attacked the individualists. The Far Right had a narrow and prejudiced conception of individual rights, and the Far Left had a pathetic faith in the sufficiency of its social claims. This clash came to a fierce head in the Canwell Committee hearing. The Right, as represented by the committee, enjoyed the arrogance of power, and inflicted its will upon its enemies.

I have wondered how sincere were the inquisitors. Were they insincere opportunists or sincere dogmatists with an archaic concept of human rights? "The great and chief end of men uniting into commonwealths," John Locke wrote in 1690, "is the preservation of their property." Locke's phrasing of natural rights, "life, liberty, and property," was changed in the Declaration of Independence, to "life, liberty, and the pursuit of happiness." When "the pursuit of happiness" was substituted for "property," Jefferson and his colleagues broadened immeasurably the concept of human rights. The Far Right never made this leap.

The broad concept of human rights only gradually took hold of the people. The American Revolutionary slogan of liberty and equality for *all* was scarcely taken seriously by the framers of the Constitution. "All" did not include women or slaves. Even the right of male suffrage was restricted by property qualifications in most states, and equality before the law was not even mentioned in the Bill of Rights. Despite the plain language of the First Amendment, free speech was severely restricted by the Sedition Act of 1798. Luther Baldwin of New Jersey, for example, was fined $150 (no small sum in those days) for hoping out loud that a cannon fired in a presidential salute would hit President Adams in the seat of his pants.

The drive for human equality scarcely began until the Civil War, but it eventually found legal expression in the Civil War amendments. Until the adoption of the Fourteenth Amendment, the Bill of Rights was held to apply only at the federal level. Because most violations of rights applied at the state level, this was in practice a very severe restriction. The Fourteenth Amendment, removing this restriction, provides that no state can "abridge the privileges or immunities of citizens of the United States; nor . . . deprive any person of life, liberty, or property, without due process of law; nor deny to any person . . . the equal protection of the laws." Despite this unequivocal language, the courts protected mainly property rights until well into the twentieth century. The broad extension in practice of due process and equal protection of the laws was the cumulative result of many Supreme Court decisions.

Equality has been the great theme in recent drives toward human rights—equality between races, between sexes, between citizens and aliens, between rich and poor, between police and suspects, between prosecutors and accused. There is now a wide and increasing consensus that special privileges are just only if they result in compensating benefits for the disadvantaged members of society. The humanist ideal is to share without stint the good things of life and to make the things shared just as good as possible.

Never in history has this ideal been more urgent than now. So long as there are vast disparities in the interpretation and fulfillment of rights, among nations, races, classes, and creeds, the danger of holocaust will persist. Nuclear war would likely bring, not the victory of either side, but the extermination of both. The right to survival—the precondition of every other right—is now inseparable from the full gamut of rights.

I wrote *False Witness* while the Vietnam War was raging and repression was mounting. Neither I nor anyone else at that time foresaw the scandals that would drive a President from office. But, in my own way, I had experienced the impact of sinister forces, and I warned my readers of the dangers that impended. The dangers have far from ceased.

There is an old saying: "The Two Sins against Hope are Presumption and Despair." Sins against hope—the *presumption* that the future is settled and that nothing need or can be done to ward off fate, the *despair* that there is no way beyond or around or through the dangers that beset us—these two sins we must resist with all our might.

Preface

IT IS strange that the critical events that I shall narrate could happen in America, and it is profoundly disturbing that they did happen. Strange it is that I, an ordinary American, was caught up in a crisis so revealing. If persons such as I were in danger, the whole country was in danger. I *was* in danger, and our country is still in danger.

The accusations of a false witness put me in jeopardy. The hearing before the Committee on Un-American Activities in which he testified is the heart of my narrative. Everything else leads up to this, grows out of it, or is a reflection on its larger significance. The false witness at this hearing is a fitting symbol not only of the forces arrayed against me but of our whole historical period. Reckless of the truth, the professional informer has been a typical product of an age of tensions and strife.

In the hearing, there were none of the protections assured by the Constitution in a court of law. The freedoms of the First and Fifth amendments were violated by the very inquisition itself. There was no judge or jury, no right of cross-examination of hostile witnesses, no right to subpoena evidence or introduce witnesses in one's own defense. Although legal counsel was allowed, the lawyers were either forbidden to speak or restricted drastically in what they could say. In contrast, the gossip and slander of witnesses "friendly" to the committee ran on without check. From the standpoint of the accused, it is paradoxical to call these proceedings a hearing, since those who wished to speak in their own defense were often not given a chance to be heard. Instead of being assumed innocent until proven guilty, they had the burden of proving their innocence. Although they were not charged with any crime and not subjected to physical harassment, many people lost their jobs, were blacklisted, and suffered in other ways (to say nothing of mental anguish) as a result of the hearing. Some were eventually thrown into prison on charges of contempt of the committee. In the absence of due process, the hearing room became a natural haven for falsehood. The fanatic's readiness to twist the truth was reinforced, and the perjurer was protected.

Two other false witnesses against me testified at a later extradition hearing. This second hearing was also shockingly irregular and unconstitutional. All proper safeguards were set aside, and the two perjurers lied as outrageously as my first accuser. Years later, a fourth witness appeared and accused me afresh. But this time the accusation was in a court of law governed by the rules of evidence, and it was not difficult to demolish the false testimony. The contrast between arbitrary procedures at the hearings and due process in the trial is highly instructive.

A single false witness might be explained away as an isolated criminal, unrelated to the inner life of American society. But the perjuries of four witnesses are not so easy to dismiss, especially when they are employed and protected by powerful agencies of state and federal government. Much of the story that I have to tell is profoundly scandalous and raises somber questions about the character of American civilization. Although my own ordeal by perjury is the focus of my narrative, its significance far transcends any personal dimensions. The story is a kind of allegory of what happens in an age of national peril when hostilities are exacerbated and freedoms are infringed.

The sense of jeopardy both to individuals and to free institutions runs throughout the book. In the beginning, a group of suspects on a university campus is in danger. As the hearing progresses this danger intensifies. Midway through the book there is a dramatic shift, and the committee and its star witness are suddenly put in jeopardy. The double peril, first to myself and others accused, and second to the committee and its perjurer, forms the principal theme of my narrative. The chapter on the Okanogan trial echoes the double threat to the accused and the accusers. All along there is the wider theme of a nation and a world in peril.

The main crisis occurred in 1948–49, and I could have written immediately thereafter, but I have postponed writing until my point of view could become steady and more detached and until later events might add a deeper significance to the narrative. As an evocation of the past that speaks directly to the concerns of the present, my story is peculiarly relevant to our troubled times.

I have taken great pains to tell the truth. My memory

has been supplemented and corrected by authentic records, such as affidavits, the findings of investigators, the official transcripts of the legislative hearing and the court, my own notes, and the notes of my attorney written shortly after the events. I have made every effort to write a narrative that will stand the scrutiny of historians.

There is another kind of truth—faithfulness to inner thoughts and convictions—that is more difficult to achieve, but I have spared no pains to be truthful in this sense also. I am writing about actions that have an inner side, consisting of processes of thought. I tell the story of these mental processes with all the honesty that I can muster. This kind of disclosure no "outsider" could write.

If the question be asked, why should I, a professor of philosophy, write so personal a narrative, the answer may be found in the words of Paul Valéry, the French poet. "I hope you will forgive this venture in self-exploration," he writes in *Variété V*. "But it seems to me a great deal more useful to describe something I have myself experienced than to simulate knowledge independent of the knowing mind, some observation from which the human observer has been banished. In truth, there is no theory which is not a fragment, and a carefully prepared fragment, of an autobiography."

I write with a sense of urgency, since my experience may help the young grasp the dangers that confront them. Perhaps they will take heart from my narrative, observing not only the power and repressiveness of the reactionary forces but the victory won by ballot, court, and free press.

Many young activists are alienated from American life and appalled by "the power structure." The gulf that separates them from the police and the politicians can be closed only by very fundamental reconstruction. But those who resort to violence may serve merely as provocateurs —as the Communist rowdies served to spur on the Nazis and seal Hitler's triumph. To the young I say, "Keep bright the arrows of the human spirit, but make sure that they are arrows of love and not hate, of Eros and not Thanatos."

My purpose in writing this book is to strengthen the forces of reason and good will. But I do not claim to belong to the party of angels, for as William Blake has said, "Angels have the vanity to speak of themselves as the only wise." There is a great deal of wisdom in a "proverb of hell" cited by Blake: "Expect poison from standing water." To combat the follies of our age, we must keep alive the dissenting devil under our skin. Mine is a book of dissent as well as a book of affirmation.

Acknowledgments

I AM indebted to Edwin Guthman, Angelo Pellegrini, Paul Coughlin, Arthur Kobler, Arval Morris, and William Dwyer, all of whom read and very helpfully criticized my manuscript, and to Professor Herbert Schneider, who has kindly granted permission for me to quote from letters written by him and his late wife Grenafore. My thanks are also extended to Holt, Rinehart, and Winston, Inc., who have allowed me to incorporate a few sentences from my book, *Ethics and the Human Community* (1964), and to the editors of *Teachers College Record*, who have given me permission to adapt a brief passage from my article, "Teaching about Communism," which appeared in the April, 1963, issue.

False Witness

1

Alarm

It was the middle of May in the year 1948. I was hard at work in my office in Savery Hall, the home of the Philosophy Department of the University of Washington in Seattle. There was a knock on my door. When I opened it I recognized two of the investigators of the Committee on Un-American Activities of the state legislature, the tall and massive Ernest P. Stith and the portly Evert Pomeroy. I had seen these men on the campus and in the halls of the university, and I knew they were investigating "subversive activities." They talked to me about an hour. "Our information," they said, "puts you in the center of the Communist conspiracy."

The investigation on the campus reflected what was happening on the world scene. In the months following the Japanese surrender and the end of World War II, the bright hope symbolized by the United Nations faded rapidly and the alliance that had defeated the Nazi-Fascist

Axis fell apart. Stalin tightened his dictatorship and broke his promise to hold free elections in the "liberated countries" of Eastern Europe. "From Stettin in the Baltic to Trieste in the Adriatic," declared Winston Churchill in the spring of 1946, "an iron curtain has descended across the Continent." A year later his words were even more dour. "What is Europe now?" he cried. "It is a rubble-heap, a charnel house, a breeding-ground of pestilence and hate." Communist revolt flared in Greece and Turkey, the Communist Party grew by leaps and bounds in Italy and France, the Russians appeared to be winning the Cold War.

Outside of Europe the conditions were no more reassuring. In Asia, in North Africa, in the Middle East, the colonial peoples were seething with revolt. Most frightening of all was the march of the Chinese Communists toward total victory. By the spring of 1947, hardheaded political analysts such as George Kennan had decided that nationalist China could not be saved. To most Americans it appeared that history was racing down the wrong track.

The American people distrusted political developments in their own country almost as much as abroad. Conservatives charged that free institutions were being strangled by bureaucracy and "creeping socialism." There was a widespread conviction that the "eggheads" were conspiring with Communists to subvert "free enterprise." Echoing popular fears, the economist Friedrich A. von Hayek in his best-seller *The Road to Serfdom* argued that New Deal liberalism and Naziism sprang from the same roots. In the congressional election of 1946 the campaign cry of the Republicans was the question, "Had enough?"

In reply, the people rose up with a hiss and elected the

first Republican Congress since the days of Herbert Hoover. Control of the Washington State Legislature fell into the hands of conservatives for the first time in fourteen years. Leaders in both parties immediately called for determined action to meet "the Communist menace." Even before the legislature convened, a caucus of senators pointed accusingly at the University of Washington. In a front-page newspaper story dated December 13, 1946, Fred Niendorff, political reporter for the *Seattle Post-Intelligencer*, quoted the caucus statement: "It is common knowledge in many quarters that the Communists have infiltrated the University of Washington campus and that their supporters have found important places on the faculty. . . . As a matter of fact, there is abundant evidence to show that besides their infiltration into labor unions and political organizations the Communists are trying everything in the book to reach American youth through the schools." In this same article, Niendorff forecast the establishment of the Committee on Un-American Activities and its investigation of the University of Washington.

Taking office in January, 1947, the new legislators promptly authorized a Joint Legislative Fact-Finding Committee on Un-American Activities to investigate subversive individuals and organizations whose purpose was to "undermine the stability of our American institutions." The committee was empowered to function after the adjournment of the 1947 legislature and was directed to report to the 1949 session.

The new committee was popularly known as the Canwell Committee after its chairman, Albert F. Canwell. Its only liberal member, Representative George Yantis, was ill at the time of his appointment and died in December, 1947, one month before the committee's first public hearing. The only other Democrat on the committee, Thomas H. Bienz, was a member of the conservative coalition in the Senate. The five Republican members of the committee, including Chairman Canwell, were all conservatives. Representative Canwell attributed his knowledge of investigative techniques to his previous experience as deputy sheriff in Spokane County. Assisting Canwell was a staff of seven investigators headed by William J. Houston, an attorney and former investigator for the United States Civil Service Commission.

From the beginning it was evident that the University of Washington would be investigated. Late in March, Senator Bienz, addressing the Spokane Realty Board, declared that there were "probably not less than 150 on the University of Washington faculty who are Communists or sympathizers with the Communist Party," and that the Canwell Committee would "name names when the time comes." At the first public hearing of the committee (an investigation of an old-age pension union) several university professors were accused of Communist affiliations. Then on April 23 the Board of Regents met with Canwell and issued an announcement "unanimously" welcoming the committee's investigation of alleged subversive activities among the faculty. Canwell publicly announced on May 4 that there would be such a hearing, and that "evidence now in the possession of the Committee concerning certain members of the University faculty will be publicized in the same manner that the Committee publicized its evidence concerning the Washington Pension Union. . . ." This meant screaming headlines in the press. By the time of Canwell's announcement, the investigators for the committee were already busy interviewing suspects and informers.

The whole campus was seething with rumors and accusations. Wherever faculty and students gathered there was intense speculation as to who might be investigated and who would act as informer. A few teachers sided with the committee, but most were opposed. Some of the oldest and most respected professors, such as Allen R. Benham and Edward G. Cox, ordered the investigators out of their offices with sharp rebuke. Many members of the faculty, at least in private, criticized the regents and the president of the university for being too compliant.

As time wore on, nerves became edgy and tempers flared. One balmy day when windows were open, the argument among a number of teaching assistants and students waxed so hot that a pistol was pulled out and brandished, and a frightened defender of the Canwell Committee jumped out of a second-story apartment window and sprained his ankle. In our Teachers' Union, which was the most left-wing faculty organization on the campus, there were fierce discussions between those who advocated unilateral defiance of the committee and those who favored cooperation with the campus chapter of the American Association of University Professors. The Washington State Federation of Teachers, with which our campus union was affiliated, called a public meeting in Seattle at which the Washington Committee on Academic Freedom was organized. This citizens' committee, with an active and dedicated staff, continued to function in defense of accused teachers for months thereafter.

The atmosphere on the campus had already become highly charged when Stith and Pomeroy knocked on my door. At first they appeared to be friendly and asked me questions about the political activities of my colleagues. I was tempted to say, "Go to hell!" but I restrained myself and replied that the role of informer was contrary to my moral code. The ensuing altercation was tense and hostile. I criticized the committee and its methods, explaining that a politically inspired investigation of the faculty was inconsistent with the freedom and dignity of a university. As the conversation drew toward a close they pressed me with questions about myself. In reply, I said I was not and had never been a member of the Communist Party, and that I disagreed with the Communists in fundamental respects.

"We know about you," they said, "and your subversive record is clear."

"You have been misinformed," I responded.

The conversation ended on this discordant note.

2

Why Had
They Knocked
on My Door?

THAT night at home and on many occasions thereafter I reviewed my past. What actions of mine had brought these men to my door? Why did I react to their questions as I did?

After reflecting, I realized that what I had done to arouse the suspicions of the Un-American Activities Committee was structured very deep in my being. It was inevitable that I should have the political convictions that brought me to this moment of peril. My ancestral background and parentage, my childhood and youth, my education at the university, my marriage to Virginia, my involvement in political causes—all these factors and more made me believe and act as I did.

My grandparents were an adventurous lot and set the family pattern of independence. I saw my grandfather Miller when I was eight or nine on a family visit to his home in Eaton, a little country town in Ohio. I can still remember him as a salty old gentleman with a flowing beard and a rich, unexpurgated vocabulary. As a lad reared in Germany, he resolved to cross the ocean and seek his fortune in America rather than submit to compulsory military training in the Kaiser's army. He saved up enough money to buy a steamship ticket, bade good-bye to his family, and sailed alone for the land of freedom. He never lost this adventurous spirit. Of my grandmother Mary I can say very little, since she died before I was born.

My paternal grandfather, Solomon Rader, was an old Indian fighter and gold miner, an almost legendary figure. In 1852, when he was twenty years old, he left his parental home, a farm in Indiana, to make the long dangerous trek to Oregon. Working his way to St. Joseph, Missouri, he joined a caravan of twenty-seven wagons, with five yoke of oxen to each wagon, transporting one hundred and fourteen men, women, and children. They were attacked by Indians, and some of their cattle and equipment was stolen en route. Six months and thirteen days after they left St. Joseph, they pulled into Jacksonville, in southwestern Oregon. After eight years of rugged pioneer life, Solomon returned to Indiana, where he became a farmer and later a storekeeper. There he married a Scottish-American lass, Martha Ann Stuart, who bore him a son, Cary Melvin Rader, my father.

Cary Melvin was faithful to the pioneer tradition. When he was twenty-three, after graduating from law school at Danville, Indiana, he traveled to Walla Walla in the distant state of Washington. I still have the letters that he wrote to his sweetheart, Harriet Miller, a young schoolteacher living in Eaton, Ohio. From these letters it appears that Walla Walla was still a frontier community.

"I see a great many Indians at this place," he wrote. "They mostly wear gaudy colored blankets and moccasins." He formed a law partnership with Miles Poindexter, later a United States Senator, and before long he felt settled and prosperous enough to marry. The ceremony took place in Harriet's home at Eaton, in late August, 1893. The young couple immediately journeyed west and were soon established in a new home in Walla Walla, where years later they were joined by Cary's parents.

Harriet was tall, slender, and rather delicate in health. In those days, when women laced themselves tightly and a slender waist was the height of style, she must have been very much in the mode. My father loved to say that when he measured her girth and compared it with the dimensions of a *very* large strawberry, once and a half around the strawberry was equal to once around my mother's waist! Delicate in personality as well as build, Harriet was serious and introspective.

When I was born in 1903, Walla Walla had about ten thousand inhabitants, and it grew to about fifteen thousand by the time I left for college in 1921. People died, but few moved away. My father and mother lived for more than forty years in the house where their three children were born. My brother Ralph, eight years my elder, ironically called me "Shorty" (I was tall for my age) and, in a big-brotherly way, was friendly. Martha, my sister, was four years older than I, but despite the difference in age we were very fond of each other. The family often went on picnics or camping trips, and I learned to love the woods while fishing or clambering up mountain paths.

Early in life I caught from Dad the contagion of political excitement. Among my oldest memories is the image of a torchlight parade—ringing a cowbell I marched with other noisy Democrats down Main Street. I shall never forget how elated we were when Woodrow Wilson won the very close presidential election of 1916. We stood for hours on a crowded street corner watching with intense interest as the returns were flashed on a screen. The next day, when the late returns from California assured Wilson's victory, I was one of the happiest persons in the world.

I shall tell just one incident to illustrate my father's political temperament. Toward the end of the first World War there was a "red scare," and Dad was involved in defending some of the victims. One day he received a telephone request to interview a prospective client in the nearby county jail. There, in one of the cells, he found a Non-Partisan League organizer from North Dakota.

The league, a semisocialist organization, was spreading like a prairie fire in the Dakotas, and the sparks were floating out to the Far West. Among conservative farmers and businessmen the league was anathema. The organizer told my father that he had been sent into the Walla Walla Valley to recruit members, that he was meeting with some success, that he had been repeatedly threatened, and that he was finally arrested on the charge of impersonating an officer.

"I have told a number of people that I used to be a deputy sheriff," he said. "This was the pretext for arresting me. I have impersonated nobody, and I want you to defend me."

"All right," my father replied, "I will defend you."

While the case was pending, another attorney in the city called him on the telephone.

"Can you come to my office?" he asked. "I want to discuss an important matter."

[12]

When my father walked into the attorney's office, he was ushered by a secretary into an inner room where, to his great surprise, a group had gathered: the minister of our church, a leading banker, a successful real-estate agent, and other substantial citizens.

"We are a Committee of Public Safety," a spokesman gravely announced after my father was seated. "We have discovered that you are defending a Red, a pro-German, a traitor. If you are a good American, you will drop the case."

My father believed in the right of an accused man to receive a legal defense. "I will not drop the case," he replied.

"We will expose you publicly," threatened the members of the committee.

"Go to hell," my father answered, and walked out.

A meeting of the local Bar Association was then called, and a motion of censure passed. Some of the members of the association stayed away from the meeting, others attended and opposed the motion, but the majority of those present voted "aye." Dad continued the case and secured the release of the organizer.

I shall always remember with what deep emotion he told me, a boy of fifteen, about these incidents. "I can no longer go to church," he said. "I keep staring at that damned minister and I see others who were also there."

After the war, at the height of the Red Scare, Father was asked to take the case of some Wobblies accused of "criminal syndicalism." There had been many arrests of "subversives" under both federal and state law. Finally a group of Wobblies who had drifted into Walla Walla Valley were seized and charged with criminal syndicalism. Dad took the case and was intensely interested in the outcome. He brought home samples of I.W.W. songs and pamphlets and told me about his conversations with the accused. "These men are illiterate," he said. "They have little idea what their organization means." They had joined the I.W.W., he said, mainly because it promised an end to ten-hour work days, lice-ridden bunks, filthy bedrolls, and underpay. Like most of the other Wobblies, they talked about the One Big Union and the way it would lift the mass of workers out of the gutter. Accused of no personal crimes, they were indicted because they belonged to a radical organization.

The trial took place during school vacation, and I attended most of the sessions. I remember the confused, inarticulate Wobblies on the stand, the argument by the prosecution that we must save our institutions from the Reds, and my father's final argument appealing to the Bill of Rights. He lost the case, and his clients were sentenced to the penitentiary.

Far from being a Communist, my father was a loyal Democrat who believed in the ancient tradition of human rights, and I deeply admired his courage and integrity.

In the autumn of 1921 I left home to enter the University of Washington. Few schools in America could boast such a stalwart band of liberal professors as J. Allen Smith in political science, Vernon Louis Parrington in American literature, William Savery in philosophy, and a number of their colleagues. All three of the men I have named were subjected to prolonged and vehement attack from conservatives during their lifetimes, but their teaching and scholarship were so distinguished that campus buildings have since been named after them.

Among the courses that affected me most deeply were Theresa McMahon's Economics of Welfare and Howard

Woolston's courses on the sociology of crime, poverty, and other social disorders; but the course that struck me hardest and almost revolutionized my life was Savery's Social Ethics. He assigned such books as John Stuart Mill's *On Liberty*, and we listened to exciting lectures on the trial and death of Socrates, the social implications of Christianity, and the ideals of socialism and liberalism. Names such as William Morris, Karl Marx, and Peter Kropotkin suddenly became very real to me. Although we learned about the great rebels, we never lost sight of the central humanistic tradition of Western civilization.

I joined a campus debate club and found congenial friends among its members. Outside of class, we were reading books like Anatole France's *Penguin Island* and Bertrand Russell's *Proposed Roads to Freedom*, and we were swapping ideas in our club or in our rooms. Supplied with good wine by Angelo Pellegrini, an Italian boy nicknamed "Pelly," we had some very gay evenings together.

Since this is a political narrative, I shall barely mention certain grave personal experiences that occurred during my college years. I developed glandular tuberculosis, and it was only after years of struggle that I regained health. More shattering than my own illness was the death of my sister Martha. This sweet and lovely girl, who was living in Seattle while I was in college, died suddenly from uremic poisoning during the autumn of my senior year. As I lay awake in the still of the night thinking of this life that had been so brief, I wondered if I could ever find a faith worth having. A faith for living! This I wanted more than anything else in the world, but it was no glib orthodoxy for which I was searching. Although Martha's death and my long illness had nothing directly to do with politics, they sobered my view of the world and sharpened the edge of my idealism. When I discovered in my teachers a devotion to freedom and social justice, I responded with a new intensity.

Late in my senior year I fell in love with a slender brunette. Both she and I were hungering for companionship, and it was not long before we were engaged. The story of our quick and impetuous marriage, our joys and difficulties and our final estrangement, is a personal narrative that I shall leave almost entirely untold.

We were very young in the autumn of 1926 when we married—Katherine was nineteen, and I was twenty-two. I could not really support a wife: although by this time I had become a graduate student and teaching fellow in philosophy, my income was very low. I was still rather sick and neurotic, and she was little more than a precocious youngster. In about a year and a half we had a son, Gordon; and for four troubled years thereafter we three lived together, experiencing triumphs and defeats.

Although I had begun my graduate work in philosophy, I finally turned to English literature. In August, 1929, I completed my doctor's thesis on Wordsworth, having already received an appointment as an assistant professor at Western Reserve University. We found the weather in Cleveland bleak, and the city dirty. During the Christmas vacation, I unexpectedly received an offer to teach in the Philosophy Department back at my Alma Mater. As I paced the floor trying to decide, the vision of Washington's lakes and mountains and evergreen forests rose in my mind's eye, and I realized too that I had never ceased to love philosophy. So we returned to Seattle, and it was there, after the beginning of the Great Depression, that Katherine and I finally parted.

For something over a year I lived with my old friend

Angelo Pellegrini in a small cottage near the university. This was a time of transition. I was seeking something, but I did not know what I was seeking. I wanted some kind of order, proportion, some kind of working harmony. I wanted to put together the scattered fragments of my life into some kind of pattern.

Then with dramatic suddenness, I fell in love again. No one ever fell, heels over head, more in love than I. It was the late spring of 1934 when this happened, and the summer that followed was the happiest time of my life. I found in Virginia Baker, an art student, a person with great tenderness and imagination. In the course of time she became a high school teacher, and during her spring vacation in 1935 we were married and enjoyed a brief honeymoon in Victoria, British Columbia.

I was very lonely when I fell in love with Virginia, and she brought to our marriage warmth of affection and subtlety of understanding. But, as the months wore on, I realized that I was not so transformed as I thought I was —deep down, I was still unwell. For Virginia, also, there were serious problems.

Her mother was over forty and her father, Dr. Albert T. Baker, over sixty at the time of her birth. During the Civil War he had run away from home and enlisted as drummer boy and later as an infantryman in the Union Army. After the war he obtained an M.D. degree from Harvard, and in 1875 he moved out to the state of Washington. There, in the frontier town of Centralia, he married, reared a family, and practiced medicine for many years before he was divorced and subsequently married again. When two daughters, Louisa and Virginia, were born from his second marriage, he was loath to assume the new burdens and withdrew into himself. He loved to steal away to his office, hang up the sign "The Doctor Is Out," and write poetry for hours behind locked doors. So little did he attend to business that the family income was low, and, to make matters worse, he was restless and moved repeatedly from one small town to another.

Contrary to her husband's convictions as a physician, Virginia's mother Effie became a Christian Scientist, refusing to permit the children to be vaccinated or to have other medical care. She sacrificed to give the two girls music lessons and other advantages, but the gnawing arthritic pain that began to plague her soon after her babies were born made life very difficult. As an intelligent, restless, ambitious woman, she must have been terribly frustrated by the illness. Her courage and stamina were remarkable, but inwardly she rankled as the disease cruelly progressed. The home atmosphere that resulted from these conditions was not happy or reassuring.

As a high school student in Portland, Virginia earned her own way by doing domestic work in homes. Later, at the University of Washington, she majored in art while working as a waitress and was almost entirely self-supporting. When she graduated the Depression had already set in, and she found it impossible to secure work either as an artist or as a teacher. She managed to live with occasional low-paid jobs, but at other times she was unemployed and desperately in need of money.

At the time we fell in love, Virginia was a waitress in a small restaurant near the campus. The following autumn she found work as a substitute teacher in the public schools, but when we married, in the spring of 1935, she was forced under existing rules to give up her teaching job. Although I was an assistant professor, my "depression salary" was little more than two hundred dollars a

[18]

month. It was no easy matter for us, as one child after another was born, to live on this salary. Just the business of stretching the income, managing the household, and rearing the children was a considerable burden. Since Gordon, the child of my first marriage, was in our custody during most of this period, Virginia and I had a little one to take care of from the very beginning of our marriage. Then we had four children of our own—Miriam born in 1937, Barbara in 1939, Cary in 1941, and David in 1943.

We rejoiced in the children, but we had to keep our noses to the grindstone. I had to work hard and to use most of my time apart from home duties on teaching and professional research. Virginia, trained as a sculptor, found it impossible to continue with her art. In addition, her mother, who was becoming ever more an invalid, stayed with us from time to time, and this involved additional burdens. Seldom could we afford help, and so unremitting were the tasks to be performed that the strain, physical and nervous, was almost more than Virginia could bear.

I have told these things about Virginia to make clear why we share a common outlook. Both of us have had enough experience of the difficulties of life so that we are distrustful of easy and simple answers. As Virginia once said to me after a rather harrowing experience, "People who simply condemn are on the outside, they never understand. They have so little sense of complexity."

Our century has been beset by the Terrible Simplifiers. They think they know the answer to life's riddles and are intolerant of those who continue to question, or whose answers are different from theirs. This is especially true in politics. Virginia and I have no taste for these simplifications.

Although my story has scarcely more than begun, I think I have already told enough to indicate why I was a militant liberal and why neither Virginia nor I could accept so simplistic an answer as Fascism or Communism. I shall tell later how I responded to the Great Depression and the mounting fury of Fascist and Nazi aggression. It will then become clear why I was visited by investigators for the Un-American Activities Committee.

3

The

Threat

Two or three weeks after the first visit by Stith and Pomeroy, they suddenly reappeared. Intercepting me as I stepped out of my office into the hall, they grinned broadly and handed me a subpoena. It "commanded" me "to attend the Joint Legislative Committee on Un-American Activities in the State of Washington" at its forthcoming inquiry into the University of Washington and "there to remain until discharged by said Committee." I soon heard that more than thirty such subpoenas had been served on various members of the university community. Included were not only faculty members and their wives but Burton and Florence James, directors of the Seattle Repertory Playhouse.

Among those who had been subpoenaed there were stormy conferences to determine upon a defense policy, but no agreement was forthcoming. One group, including Professor Herbert Phillips in my own department, announced that they would not respond to the subpoenas. Later this group decided to appear at the hearing but to withhold crucial answers on the stand. Another group, to which I belonged, decided to answer truthfully questions about themselves but to refuse to incriminate others. This group engaged Ed Henry, a liberal Seattle attorney, to advise and represent them.

Early in July I had an interview with Raymond B. Allen, the president of the university. He was a middle-aged man of impressive stature and build, and I felt tense as I faced him in his stately office. I told him the truth about myself, and he advised me to have a talk with Canwell and Houston to clear up misunderstandings.

I followed his advice. After telephoning for an appointment, I went down to the Armory Building where the committee had established its headquarters. I found Mr. Houston, rather dark in complexion and large in build, waiting for me in an inner office. Soon I was aware of another person in the room sitting at a desk within earshot. This slender, quiet person about forty years of age was later introduced to me as Chairman Canwell. In response to Houston's questions, I stated that I had never been a member of the Communist Party and that my activities in the United Front organizations had been motivated by democratic and humanitarian principles.

Houston replied, "We will call two witnesses that will testify that you were present at closed Communist meetings."

Then he mentioned a star witness who would testify. This man, he said, had been a high-ranking member of the Communist Party and had even conferred with Stalin. Since I knew no such person I was puzzled.

Houston continued, "Two students will report that in

one of your classes you praised the Constitution of the Soviet Union as the most wonderful statement of principles that you have ever read." I replied that this accusation would be ridiculous.

Houston said that the committee had worked out a detailed chart of my activities and that I had invariably followed the Communist Party line. I told him this was a mistaken view, and I mentioned respects in which I had disagreed with the Communists.

"Teachers are going to be fired at the university because of the committee's hearing," Houston threatened. "They will be unable to find new teaching positions elsewhere."

On the point of leaving I turned and addressed Canwell directly. I said that I would be glad if the committee would find out the real facts about me. Then I gave him the names of ten people who knew me intimately and asked that they be questioned. I had carefully selected the names of these ten because they all knew very well that I was not a Communist. Included were some of my oldest and best friends. Others named knew me less intimately, but they had heard me criticize the Communist Party and the Soviet Union. Houston wrote down these names and admitted that I had listed men of good repute. On checking later, I discovered that not one of them was ever approached by the committee or its investigators.

When I told my attorney, Ed Henry, about my interview with Houston and Canwell he scolded me roundly. "It is dangerous," he said, "to talk in the absence of a friendly witness." Later I recalled this admonition at a crucial moment.

Although I was not surprised to have been subpoenaed, I was deeply shocked by this inverview in the office of the committee. By innuendo if not by express statement, Houston had threatened to disgrace me and to force my discharge from the university. Several times he referred to witnesses who would identify me as a Communist. Then there was the enigmatic reference to a star witness who had interviewed Stalin. I saw no connection between this man and myself, but it was strange and perhaps a little disturbing that he was mentioned. The whole conversation had a quality of nightmarish unreality, as if it were an episode in a Kafka novel.

Privately the committee and its chief investigator must have had doubts about any very serious charges against me. On the eve of the hearing Houston told Henry that neither he nor his associates believed that I was a Communist, but that I would be forced to sit through the sessions and "sweat it out" as a form of punishment. The *Seattle Times* later reported (October 21, 1949) that the committee members "did not believe that Rader was a Communist. . . . The committee believed, however, that Rader could give considerable information about Communist activity on the campus but had not done so. It was decided to subpoena Rader and force him to sit through the hearing in the hope that he would 'break.' "

I was determined not to join the ranks of the informers. They had played a wicked role in the totalitarian states and were poisoning public life in America.

4

United

Front

WHY was I being threatened? Was it simply that the committee and its investigators thought they could extort information from me? Or was I, without being a Communist, a "fellow traveler" who could be mistaken for a member of the Party? Or could I, despite all my disclaimers, be a crypto-Communist? I shall answer as honestly as I can.

I was deeply stirred by the Depression and the Nazi-Fascist movement, and I responded to these tragic events with the determination to do all I could to avert catastrophe. Knowing that I was powerless and insignificant as a single individual, I joined with others in the "United Front." There was nothing unique in what I was doing— millions all over the world were doing likewise. But I may have attracted more attention than most local participants since I never concealed my views or activities.

Our family suffered less from the Depression than a

great many. Still, it was a considerable shock when my father lost most of his money and possessions. He was attorney for and director of the Peoples State Bank in Walla Walla, and he had invested rather heavily in its stocks. When the bank failed, he was legally responsible as both director and stockholder. Worst of all, the president of the bank, a close personal friend, was either killed by an intruder or committed suicide. These events had a sharp personal impact upon us, but were only a reflection of the national disaster.

Although politicians and businessmen predicted the quick return of prosperity, conditions kept on deteriorating. The failures of banks and business establishments reached panic proportions; breadlines grew longer and longer; innumerable farmers picketed to prevent mortgage foreclosures; there were many hunger strikes, and some even starved to death. "In the wet hay of leaking barns," as John Steinbeck wrote, "old people curled up in corners and died that way, so that the coroners could not straighten them out." In desperation, an "army" of poverty-stricken veterans marched on the nation's capital and encamped on the outskirts of the city, but the regulars under General Douglas MacArthur dispersed them with bayonets and burned their tents.

These were some of the conditions in the election year of 1932 when "the everybody that was nobody" won a smashing victory at the polls. Within twenty-four hours of Roosevelt's inauguration, the German Reichstag passed the Enabling Act conferring absolute power upon Adolf Hitler as chancellor of the Reich. A new era had begun!

In the state of Washington, there was a kind of revolution. The old familiar figures were swept from office, and a motley group of liberals and radicals was swept in. The city of Seattle churned with new ideas, movements, leaders. Organizations grew and proliferated with startling rapidity: the Technocrats, the Edward Bellamy Clubs, the Townsendites, the Unemployed Citizens' League, the Workers' Alliance, the Commonwealth Builders, the followers of Upton Sinclair's "Epic Plan," the Socialists, the Communists, and, among the fascistically inclined, the Silver Shirts and the Sentinels.

The new leaders were a vivid crew. There was John Dore—a witty, clever, opportunistic, hard-drinking Irishman—elected mayor after he publicly announced that he was in favor of taking the huge fortunes away from those who had stolen them from the workers of America. He later sharply reversed his position, threatening to use machine guns if necessary to keep the unemployed from rioting. There was young Marion Zioncheck, the new congressman, brilliant, eccentric, radical, whose strenuous career ended in a suicide leap from a Seattle office window, after he hastily scribbled a note, "My only hope was to improve the condition of an unfair economic system. . . ." There was Vic Meyers, Seattle jazz-band leader, who conducted a burlesque campaign for the City Council dressed as Mahatma Gandhi and later found himself, to everybody's surprise, lieutenant governor and one of the leaders of the Left Wing. There was John C. Stevenson, radio barker for the Painless Parker Dental Offices, who was denounced by Dore as an ally of "agitators, anarchists, and Russian agents" and was nevertheless elected county commissioner. There was Howard Costigan, a young, dapper, tireless, and very articulate spokesman for the socialistic "Commonwealth Builders," which later evolved into the Washington Commonwealth

Federation. There were liberals like George Yantis of Olympia, Ben Kizer of Spokane, and Irving Clark of Seattle—prominent citizens who championed civil liberties and defended the "New Deal."

Far more commanding than any local figure was the new President, Franklin D. Roosevelt. His inaugural address was bold and clear: "I favor as a practical policy the putting of first things first. . . . Our greatest primary task is to put people to work. . . . We do not distrust the future of essential democracy. The people of the United States have not failed. . . . The only thing we have to fear is fear itself."

The problem that the "progressives" faced was no easy one. It was an enormously difficult task to fashion and push through reforms adequate to put sixteen million people back to work. The supporters of the New Deal were divided about many things and especially about distant objectives. Many felt that it was a mistake to debate remote ends if agreement could be reached on immediate goals. *Unity* was the slogan of the "United Front," and unity was highly essential for success.

If unity was imperative in domestic politics, it seemed even more necessary in foreign policy. This was the period of accelerating Fascist aggression, when the threat of totalitarian enslavement and war loomed more and more ominously, and the democracies, as if motivated by a strange death wish, surrendered to Nazi-Fascist threats. The Japanese armies invaded Manchuria; Hitler denounced the Versailles Treaty and rearmed at breakneck speed; Mussolini defied the League of Nations and crushed Ethiopia; Italian and German Fascists rushed to the aid of Franco's rebellion; Japanese troops again overran China; German soldiers seized Austria and mounted an assault against Czechoslovakia. The program of appeasement, culminating in the Munich Pact, far from checking these events, encouraged new waves of blackmail, treaty-breaking, and aggression.

While these ominous events were occurring, there was one voice that rang out with singular force and clarity. Explain it however you will, Maxim Litvinov, as the spokesman of Soviet foreign policy, eloquently denounced the policy of appeasement and insisted, time and again, that only a united force could halt the Fascists. Typical of many speeches were his remarks at the sixteenth plenum of the League of Nations on July 1, 1936: "I would propose that the Covenant be adapted not to the frame of mind of one or another category of people, one or another group of statesmen, one or another group of temporary rulers, but to the frame of mind of the millions, the masses in all countries and continents, those who rightly call themselves 'mankind' and demand that peace be preserved at all costs and defended with all means. . . . We must seek to make the League universal, but we must not by any means make it safe for the aggressor. . . . To strengthen the League of Nations is to abide by the principle of collective security, which is . . . a practical measure towards the security of all peoples, to abide by the principle that peace is indivisible!"

This was the point: peace is indivisible! This was the rallying cry of the People's Front, and this was the cry that appealed most deeply to me. Peace is indivisible, and only pooled security can guarantee it. As international events rushed toward a tragic climax, millions of us felt it imperative to rally as large a force as possible behind the policy of collective security.

From time to time in human affairs there arise supreme

emergencies when the values that great masses of men hold in common are in jeopardy. Then narrower loyalties —the bonds of race, creed, nationality, party, and class— must be subordinated to that still wider and more basic loyalty—the partnership that we call mankind. It is no accident, for example, that in wartime there are coalitions within governments and among resistance groups. When faced by conflict with a great and common enemy, factions compose their differences and concentrate upon the major task. They may not have found any real solution of the issues that divide them, but emphasis upon these issues during a period of severe struggle would catastrophically divide and weaken their powers.

The United Front was a drive to forge this wider bond of unity. It was an attempt to get millions of people to act together in the face of a supreme emergency, although they belonged to different political camps and professed different ideological creeds. Such a coalition, we believed, was the only way of preventing the second World War. It alone promised to confront the aggressors with such a massive resistance that war would be too risky. If armed conflict nevertheless should come, a united front would contribute mightily to anti-Fascist victory, and, without such unity, terrible defeat was altogether possible. Such considerations impelled many millions of non-Communists like myself to join the Front Populaire in France, the Frente Popular in Spain, the United Front organizations in England and America, and similar coalitions in other lands.

It is perfectly true that there were Communists in these organizations, but the Communists looked very different then from the way they appeared in later years. Their international spokesman was Maxim Litvinov, and they were ostensibly supporting the Roosevelt administration. Like millions of others, I reasoned that a good cause should not be deserted merely because Communists supported it, and that it was no great tragedy that the Communists, who represented internationally an immense force, were combining with liberal and democratic groups in a united stand against Fascism and war. Far more disastrous, it seemed to me, would be the opposite policy of teaming up with the aggressors. I observed that there was scarcely a liberal organization anywhere in the land that did not include Communists within it. Even the Democratic party, especially in the state of Washington, was a kind of united front organization, including a most serried array of adherents, some of them conservative but others far to the left. It seemed apparent that if I refused to function in an organization simply because Communists were in it, I would be stymied, unable effectively to support the very causes that I *knew* to be right. I felt that action was imperative, and that organizations such as the American League against War and Fascism provided a program to which I was deeply committed.

These were the reasons that impelled me to devote myself arduously to the United Front. My first active participation was in the University of Washington Teachers' Union. During the initial upsurge of the New Deal, locals of the American Federation of Teachers were established at many colleges and universities, and the response on our campus was immediate and enthusiastic. More than one hundred teachers joined, and we had well-attended meetings where we discussed not only academic problems but all sorts of political questions. Sometimes we lent support to labor unions that were engaged in strikes or other struggles. On occasion, we passed resolu-

[31]

tions supporting what we regarded as progressive causes, and our secretary was busy communicating our sentiments to our congressmen or other officials. In course of time, I became a member of the executive board, a delegate to the Washington State Federation of Teachers, and, for a year, president of our campus local.

An organization in which I participated less actively was the Washington Commonwealth Federation. This represented a coalition of many different groups—the remnants of the Unemployed Citizens League, the Commonwealth Builders, the Workers' Alliance, the Technocrats, the Townsend Clubs, and various labor unions and cooperatives. Organized in 1935, it functioned for four or five years as a potent political force, endorsing Democratic candidates in state primaries and general elections and campaigning for selected candidates in Seattle's "non-partisan" municipal elections. Its executive secretary, Howard Costigan, won a wide popular audience with his facile radio broadcasts. Although the Communists were formally barred from membership, they infiltrated the organization and achieved more and more control. My association with the federation was not a close one. I never served as an officer or went regularly to its meetings, and occasionally I felt disgusted with its policies, as when it endorsed the demagogue, John C. Stevenson, as candidate for governor in the 1936 Democratic primaries.

One of the exciting events that enlisted my support was the strike that broke out on August 13, 1936, at William Randolph Hearst's *Post-Intelligencer* plant.* The news-

* Here and in much that I say later I may seem to cast reflections on the *Seattle Post-Intelligencer*. I am writing about what happened more than twenty years ago, and my remarks should not be interpreted as an attack upon the present policies of the newspaper.

[32]

paper had discharged a drama and music critic, Everhardt Armstrong, and a photographer, Frank Lynch. According to the management, it was because of incompetence and insubordination, but according to the men, it was because of their activity in the American Newspaper Guild. There were only twenty-seven members of the guild out of a total of several hundred employees, but when they decided to strike, the popular response was enormous. The Seattle Labor Council promptly supported the strikers; and longshoremen, seamen, teamsters, warehousemen, and even teachers and housewives joined in the fray. In all Seattle history there had never been such a popular strike or a more enthusiastic picket line. Mayor Dore declared that Mr. Hearst was "Public Enemy Number One," and Dave Beck, the powerful leader of the Teamsters, threw his full support to the strikers. The presses stopped, bricks flew, men were beaten, and the *Post-Intelligencer* published not a single paper until it capitulated fifteen weeks later.

Our University of Washington Teachers' Union supported the strike, and some of our members joined the picket line. This kind of participation was not to my taste, but, when I was asked by the strike committee to speak at a public meeting, I did so gladly. The mass meeting was in Ballard, a working-class district, and the audience was large and vociferous. I was one of eight or nine speakers, each representing a different segment of public opinion. I spoke as an individual citizen defending the right of employees to join labor unions of their own choosing.

The event of that time which stirred me most profoundly was the Civil War in Spain. I was a subscriber to the *New York Times* when the Fascist rebellion broke out in July, 1936, and the reports in this great newspaper stimulated me to study the whole background of the war. The Spanish Popular Front government, I soon gathered, was far from being Communist or even Socialist. At the time the revolt began, the cabinet was entirely Republican, with no Communists or Socialists. The Communists had won only 14 seats out of the 473 in the Cortes, and there were only 50,000 Communists in the country. The cry that Franco was "saving" Spain from Communism was a lie, and the effect of the revolt was precisely opposite—the rapid growth of Communism in Spain was a reaction to the rebellion.

I was excited by the larger meaning of the Civil War. I felt that Spain had become the center and focus of the greatest struggle of the age. If the Fascist dictators— Franco, Mussolini, and Hitler—had their way in Spain, a second World War would be almost inevitable; but if the republic and its friends could rally enough support, the principle of united resistance to aggression might be victorious and World War II prevented. So I did my best to help the Republican cause.

My interest in Spain was intensified by a public mass meeting in the late autumn of 1936. A delegation from the Spanish government consisting of Don Marcelino Domingo, Minister of Education, Father Sarasola, a Franciscan friar, and Isabel de Palencia, a representative at the League of Nations Assembly, was on tour of the United States and stopped in Seattle to plead the Loyalist cause. Domingo and Sarasola were impressive, but Isabel de Palencia was intensely moving. Tall, gaunt, and severe, with coal-black hair parted in the middle and combed back tightly, she spoke with such eloquence and passion that my spine tingled.

I lent my name as a sponsor to the Medical Bureau to

Aid Spanish Democracy and helped to organize several public meetings in aid of the Loyalist cause. I also worked zealously as a member of the executive board of our Seattle branch of the American League against War and Fascism, whose policy was strongly to support Republican Spain. From time to time, I spoke on the radio or at public meetings in defense of the Loyalists.

These activities provoked attack. An amusing but ominous episode occurred in June of 1937. A student Philosophy Club held a campus meeting at which a liberal, a Fascist, and a Communist presented their contrasting "political philosophies." The speakers were Francis Wilson, a member of the Political Science Department, who represented the liberal position; the editor of a local Italian-American newspaper, who defended Mussolini and the Fascist cause; and Morris Raport, a district organizer for the Communist Party. The meeting was lively and interesting. I attended out of curiosity, but had nothing to do with suggesting or arranging the meeting.

Nevertheless, the Sentinels, a small Fascist organization in the state, seized upon this opportunity to attack me. On June 15, they published a lurid mimeographed "news report" entitled the *Northwest Messenger*. This "report" omitted all reference to the appearance of Wilson and the newspaper editor, blamed the meeting upon me, and included anti-Semitic slurs against Raport. The following is a quotation from their news sheet:

"For the first time in the history of the University of Washington an alien enemy revolutionist was the invited guest speaker to address members of the student body. Morris Raport, Pacific Northwest leader of the Communist Party, spoke before the Philosophy Club in the University's Guggenheim Hall on Thursday, June 3, 1937, on the invitation of Professor Melvin Rader of the Philosophy Department of the University of Washington. The meeting was an 'open meeting.' Raport is a professional revolutionist in the pay of the Communist International. He was born in 1894 in the Tchernigoff Province in the village of Unetcha, Soviet Russia. His people were Jewish kosher butchers and cattle dealers. Morris, himself, was apprenticed as a Jewish kosher butcher."

In Walla Walla a day or two later, a man shoved a copy of the paper containing this article into my father's office and distributed other copies throughout the business district. My brother Ralph discovered that the libelous sheets had been peddled by a leader of the Sentinels, who owned an electrical appliance store. More spirited than discreet, Ralph demanded an explanation and, when he did not receive one, socked the fellow in the jaw. I heard no more about the incident until the Canwell Committee issued its printed report to the State Legislature in January, 1949. There in the appendix was reproduced, as part of its "evidence" of my subversive activities, the "news report" Herold had distributed. There was no indication in the report of the Canwell Committee that the source of this "news" was an extreme right-wing organization.

Despite such incidents, my interest in politics was unflagging. During the Munich crisis in September, 1938, Virginia and I hugged the radio to hear every snatch of news. Unforgettable was Hitler's harangue in the great Sport Palace, when he lashed his audience into a frenzied demonstration against the Czech people, their president, and any power that would dare befriend them. "The surge of voices," declared one observer, sounded like "a menagerie where all the animals had gone mad, but by some trick could be made to bay and howl in unison."

When Prime Minister Chamberlain capitulated at Munich we were dismayed. Not only had Czechoslovakia been betrayed but the Nazis had been strengthened immeasurably. The public in Seattle was greatly excited by what had happened, and when Harold Laski, as a visiting professor at the university, discussed the international situation in a series of lectures in Meany Hall, the response was amazing. Although the auditorium held several thousand people, other thousands were turned away for want of seats. After the first two or three lectures, the audience gathered several hours in advance to be sure of a place to sit. Never before had such intense interest in world politics been manifested. When Laski stood before an audience, with elaborate periodic sentences rolling limpidly from his tongue, I thought I had never before heard anyone so eloquent. His fiery denunciation of appeasement confirmed my strongest convictions; and I was therefore happy when I could help in organizing a downtown mass-meeting at which he spoke for the benefit of Loyalist Spain. The large theater that we rented for the occasion was densely packed, but the military scales had already tipped decisively in favor of Franco.

I lost two close friends in the Spanish War. Jim Norie was a man of about my own age, with an agile mind and a rather sardonic view of the world. In the Depression period, he had not succeeded in becoming established in teaching or any other job. He drifted into the Communist Party out of idealism and a sense of frustration, and the Spanish conflict moved him deeply. One day he called at our home and chatted with Virginia and me in an apparently relaxed mood. He had learned a little trick of tying a string into a complicated pattern and then untying it deftly, and he showed us this trick with an air of frivolous detachment. Secretly he had joined the International Brigade and had come to see us before leaving for Spain. He fought in one of the great battles and was killed in action.

My other friend, Thane Summers, was considerably younger than I. He had been a major in philosophy—a very earnest and idealistic student. Although he had been dating a beautiful girl, we used to say jokingly that he was too much in love with mankind in general to be very much in love with any girl in particular. He had broken all ties with his father, a conservative attorney, and had become excited about radical social philosophy. After several years he dropped out of school, partly because he was having a financial struggle and partly because he was restless and wanted to take part directly in social action. Only once did he seek my advice, and then I told him to do everything possible to finish his education.

One day he knocked at the door of our home and explained that he would like to sell us a recording of Chopin's Sonata in B-flat minor for Pianoforte, played by Percy Grainger. We opened the album and tried out the record on our phonograph, excited by Grainger's rendition and the beauty of the composition. After we bought the album, Thane tarried as if wanting to tell us something. But he confided nothing, and I did not suspect that he was scraping together money to leave for Spain. He operated a tank in the Abraham Lincoln Brigade and was mowed down in one of the fierce battles of the war. On many occasions thereafter we opened the Chopin album and listened to the stately funeral march that forms the third movement. Did Thane anticipate his own death when he brought to us this death march?

These men, Jim Norie and Thane Summers, had the courage of their convictions, and like many others they struggled to stem the Nazi-Fascist tide. I respected them for their devotion to what they believed to be right even though I disagreed with their Communism. Those of us who stayed at home tried also in our measure to prevent World War II.

In retrospect, I still think that the ideal of the United Front was absolutely sound. If it had succeeded it would have saved the world from incalculable misery, but it was betrayed by the appeasers and the Communists alike. The pact between Hitler and Stalin in the summer of 1939 was the culmination of treachery that had been present from the beginning.

I do not deny that I made mistakes during the period of the United Front. It was some time before I realized that the Party joined united fronts in order to turn them into *Communist* fronts—that often it worked clandestinely, operating through secret members, to seize control from within. Being disciplined and single-minded, they were able to transform many fine organizations into narrow pockets of orthodoxy. When liberals and socialists joined united fronts they ordinarily did so in a democratic spirit, with no intention of manipulating or dominating the unified forces, but the Communists schemed and plotted to capture these organizations. This represented a betrayal of the other parties and the essential ideal of the People's Front.

I was slow in realizing these facts. Too intense in my political commitments to see things with cold objectivity, I had not learned to look at myself or the world around me with humor or detachment. I saw the evils of depression and war very clearly, but I did not so clearly perceive the difficulties involved in creating a brave new world.

With respect to one very fundamental point I made no

mistake. Much as I liked and admired some of my Communist friends personally, I felt that there was a gulf that separated us. The nature of this cleavage is illustrated by a revealing incident. In June, 1944, the Quakers in Seattle conducted a conference on international affairs. Among the distinguished group of speakers was Bertram D. Wolfe, author of books on art and politics and a sharp critic of the Communist Party. His lecture was open to the public and widely advertised. But when the time came for him to speak in the packed auditorium, he was subjected to such a barrage of catcalls and imprecations that the meeting turned into a kind of bedlam. As the chairman strove to restore order, the din only increased in fury, and it was impossible to go on with the meeting. The Communists planted in the audience had staged a near-riot.

The next day I happened to meet a Communist friend. Although neither he nor I had been present at the meeting, we differed sharply in our reaction to the news report. I was incensed, and I told him so. He hotly retorted that Wolfe was a Trotskyite (the worst of sins) and a traitor to the anti-Nazi cause.

"How do you know?" I replied. "In any event, I believe in Wolfe's right to speak, and the right of the audience to hear him."

"He is a traitor," my friend reiterated. "He should be under arrest, and if the police won't perform their duty, he should be prevented from speaking by any means available."

These remarks precipitated an intense argument. Before it was over we were both deeply shaken; and I realized that, however much we might agree about some things, there was a world of difference between us.

He believed the Communist cause so luminously right that an outright adversary, such as Bertram Wolfe, must be sinister and vicious, and that civil liberties had no application to such persons. In a sense, he believed in democracy and thought that the Soviet Union was the most democratic of all countries; but this kind of "democracy," as he approvingly noted, denied civil liberties and democratic rights to anti-Communists. Looking at the Soviet Union in the light of his sectarian ideals, he found no invincible difficulty in accepting the monolithic police state and "the dictatorship of the proletariat." It was here that I differed.

I was as devoted as he to the ideal of a classless humanity, but I could not agree with him as to the way to achieve this objective. It seemed to me that the *means* employed by the Communists, in their daily impact upon the world, were far more important than the remote ends they professed. Even though I was radical in my conception of *ends*, I was liberal in my conception of *means*.

This fact is indicated in an exchange of letters that followed the publication of my book, *No Compromise*, a philosophical study of the conflict between democracy and Fascism. The book, brought out in midsummer 1939 by the Macmillan Company, was chosen by the English Left Book Club as their Book-of-the-Month for the following October. Victor Gollancz, the British publisher for the club, wrote to me expressing his satisfaction with the choice. He ended his letter as follows: "I am the more interested in your book, inasmuch as I have been talking to one or two people here about the desirability of founding some informal association of men and women who are pledged uncompromisingly to three things—

"1. The abolition of production for private profit.

"2. The preservation of the spirit of scepticism.

"3. The preservation of Christian ethics."

In my letter of reply I stated: "I heartily agree with you as to the desirability of founding an informal association of men and women pledged uncompromisingly to the three principles you mention. . . . If you mean to recruit members in the United States, please count me in."

I accepted the goal of a decentralized socialist economy while clinging to the basic values of Western civilization. I was no Greek humanist or Orthodox Christian, but I believed in Socratic inquirism and Christian charity. The Communists, whatever they might say, did not.

It was this body of convictions, rather than lack of invitation, that kept me out of the Communist Party. One evening in 1934, when I was alone in my home, there was a knock at the door, and when I opened it, I was greeted by a teacher-friend. I made him welcome, and we had a brief conversation.

"I have come to invite you to join the Communist Party," he said. We then discussed the matter briefly.

It seemed that all my previous life had prepared me for an answer. My father's intransigent liberalism had inspired my own liberal tendencies. My long illness, the death of my sister, the unhappiness of my first marriage, had given me a taste of sadness and quickened my sympathy for human suffering. My favorite teachers—men such as Parrington and Savery and J. Allen Smith—had strengthened my attachment to the liberal tradition. The experience of teaching social philosophy had clarified my concepts of freedom and democracy. I was an American in search of a way—but it was not the Communist way.

"No," I said, "I won't join the Communist Party."

Later I was invited into the ranks by Bob Roberts, a Communist organizer who was active in the University District. He was persistent and visited me repeatedly; but I always refused, and he finally realized that my refusal was final.

Here, then, is the truth, as frank and honest as I can make it. The story in itself would be worthless were it not representative of what many other people have experienced.

Like so many others I ran afoul of an un-American activities committee. It was a tawdry imitation of the national committee, but it shared its blindness. I could not hope that the Canwell Committee would understand the complex considerations that shaped my political convictions and prompted my activities. It was too indiscriminate in its judgments and too unprincipled in its methods. In view of the forthright stands I had taken, it was not surprising that I had incurred the committee's suspicions.

I have tried to explain how liberals like myself aroused the hostility of the right wing. Perhaps the explanation will be illuminating to those who came of age during the Cold War and have known Communists only as "the enemy." These young people of today may find it difficult to comprehend why so many liberals of my generation joined with Communists to stem the tide of disaster, and why so many others, for a time, actually became Communists. It takes a difficult feat of historical imagination for the young to understand the desperation of the Depression years and the overwhelming threat of Nazi and Fascist barbarism, or to recapture the fervor and idealism with which we rallied to the United Front. This whole chapter has been an attempt at explanation—mainly by example —of why so many answered the call.

To our latter-day critics who condemn us for the stands we took, I would reply: learn from our misadventures whatever you can. Charge us with our failures and do better in your turn. But do not suppose that criticism excuses inaction, or that it is easy for a later generation to understand the dilemmas of an earlier one.

5

The

Committee

in Session

As THE date for the hearing approached I would have been in a sanguine mood were it not for the threat hanging over me. The Board of Regents had recently promoted me from the rank of associate professor to that of professor. I had also been appointed as a visiting professor for the second session of summer school at the University of California at Los Angeles, and I planned to fly down to my new job as soon as the hearing was over. Finally, I had been awarded a research grant by the Rockefeller Foundation to study the concept of historical crisis, and I had been granted a leave of absence from the University of Washington for the autumn quarter to devote full time to this study. I expected to spend most of my leave working at the Hoover Library at Stanford University. The concept of crisis, which had already figured in my research and writing, seemed to me an exciting subject.

In still other ways fortune appeared to be smiling. We

had recently sold our home in the country and moved to a new location on the edge of Ravenna Park in the University District. We awoke to the sound of birds, and from our breakfast table we could watch the squirrels—wonderful little acrobats—leaping from branch to branch and tree to tree. Our back yard was full of salal, ferns, wild currants, and other native foliage. Almost every day I took a walk in the park either alone or with Virginia and the children. We loved our new home and the ravine. Although I was forty-four years of age, I was feeling almost boyish.

Even the prospect of the hearing hardly dampened my spirits. It would soon be over, and I would be flying south to Los Angeles. The "worst" that could truthfully be said about me was that I had participated in United Front organizations, such as the American League against War and Fascism. I felt proud of this record and prepared to defend it. If someone were to call me a Communist I felt I could rebut the charge, at least through other channels than the committee hearing.

Apart from my personal fortunes, however, I was apprehensive that the university and members of its staff would be greatly damaged. I knew enough about such committees, especially the Tenney Committee in California and the national Committee on Un-American Activities, to realize that they could be extremely unfair. In its earlier hearing on the Washington Pension Union, the Canwell Committee had followed the usual procedures of these bodies. Any lawyer who tried to defend his client, or offered an objection to the form or substance of any question, or sought to cross-examine a hostile witness, was curtly silenced. Accused persons, denied the means of testing the recollection, veracity, or personal prejudice of witnesses, had to listen in silence to whatever slander might be spoken. Similarly the public, which had the right not to be deceived, was denied the benefit of objective fact-finding procedures. The committee appeared less concerned with any legitimate legislative aim than with "trial" of its victims by screaming headlines in the press. To make matters worse, the committee's methods were being used in the sensitive area of speech and association supposedly protected by the Bill of Rights. Such bodies as the Canwell Committee were undermining the foundation of our democracy—for the rights guaranteed by the Constitution would be greatly impaired if politicians were allowed to do indirectly what the courts and police were forbidden to do directly.

It seemed appropriate that the hearing should be held in the massive stone structure of the 146th Field Artillery, with armed guards stationed at various points. In the packed hearing room Chairman Canwell gaveled the committee and the crowd to order with military dispatch. One could easily imagine that the scene was that of a court-martial, with the uniformed members of the state patrol ready to suppress any strong dissent. At a long elevated table facing the audience sat Canwell, flanked on both sides by members of his committee. A little in front of this table, on the side of the room near the windows, was a witness stand, with a chair placed alongside for the witness' attorney. Immediately in front of Canwell, in the center of the room, was a large table around which were grouped committee counsel William J. Houston, his chief assistant John Whipple, and a court reporter. On the opposite side of the room from the witness stand there was a press box with seats for reporters for the local newspapers, the national news services, and the radio stations.

[47]

This section of the room was separated by a railing from the seats set aside for the subpoenaed witnesses and, behind them, for whatever part of the public was able to cram into the room. A large overflow crowd was accommodated in a downstairs auditorium, with the sound piped in from the microphones upstairs. As witnesses mounted the stand or someone was ejected by the armed patrol, the photographers' flashbulbs would pop, and pictures would appear later in the newspapers. Pickets, carrying large hand-painted signs, marched back and forth outside the building.

Chairman Canwell opened the hearing by explaining that no nonsense would be permitted. "We will proceed with proper dignity here," he said. "No demonstrations will be tolerated, no speeches from the audience; any violations of these instructions will be summarily dealt with. We intend to have an orderly procedure here at all cost." He then explained that the attorneys for the subpoenaed witnesses would be allowed to act in an advisory capacity only. "They may freely advise their clients whether or not to answer; they may not argue before this hearing. We are not going to debate any of the issues regarding the constitutionality of this committee, or its method of procedure." Then there was the rollcall of the subpoenaed witnesses, and each of us answered to his name.

The first witness, Moro Jewell, identified himself as a private detective and a former employee of the Army Intelligence Service. He testified that in the latter capacity he had joined the Communist Party, and he named several members of the faculty as having been members.

The second witness was Professor Sophus Winther of the English Department at the university. He identified himself as an ex-Communist who had withdrawn from the Party in 1946, and named eight teachers who had been his Party associates. When Houston interrogated him about me he replied: "I recall Melvin Rader being discussed—and . . . I think they thought it would be desirable to get him into the Party, but he refused. And I think, what they didn't realize was that he drew a very sharp line between accepting the Communist philosophy and that of an honest liberal." Mr. Houston then asked: "You would class Professor Melvin Rader as an honest liberal then, in 1936?" Dr. Winther replied, "Yes, I would." Houston's mention of the date 1936 struck me as a little sly. The witness had suggested no such time limitation.

Winther also was asked whether he had been given the assignment to recruit me into the Communist Party, and he answered, "No—I—no, I don't think I did." This response recalled to my mind a conversation a few days before. At an opportune moment, I had drawn him aside to check my hazy recollection that it was he that had once invited me to join the Party, but he denied that he had ever so approached me. Later when I myself was on the stand I recalled this denial.

After a brief interrogation of Mrs. Winther, Houston called to the stand one of his "expert witnesses," Mr. J. B. Matthews from New York City. Under questioning, Matthews described himself as formerly "the leading fellow traveler in the United States." In his very lengthy testimony, he supplied a list of some 230 "Communist front" organizations currently operating, and declared that 1,000 such fronts had existed. Named among the "fellow travelers" were such famous men as Albert Einstein, Harold Urey, Frederic March, Arthur Schlesinger, Jr., and Senator Charles W. Tobey. He condemned the new president of Columbia University, Dwight D. Eisenhower, for harboring "several hundred fellow travelers" on the campus, and for accepting a $30,000 gift from the government of Poland to establish a chair in Polish language and literature.

On Tuesday morning one of the subpoenaed professors, Garland Ethel of the English Department, told me that he was scheduled to testify in the afternoon and that it might be helpful to cite some Biblical passages against "tale-bearing" and "scandal-mongering." So as soon as the noon recess began I telephoned Madeleine Carroll, the English Department librarian, and asked her to look up in a Biblical concordance a number of such passages. At the end of the recess I called her back, and she dictated to me several quotations, such as Paul's denunciation of "tattlers" and "busybodies" (I Timothy 5:13). These quotations I handed to Ethel.

When he was called to the stand, he testified that he had been a Party member but had severed connections in 1941. Despite the threat of imprisonment for contempt, he refused again and again to name his Party associates. "My own particular code of honor," he said, "forbids that kind of naming of persons to their possible injury." In the excitement of testifying, he forgot to quote from the Bible and instead cited Polonius' advice to his son: "This above all, to thine own self be true, and it must follow as the night the day, thou can'st not then be false to any man." On this point of honor Professor Ethel refused to budge. The next morning he was recalled to the stand and again threatened with contempt, but he categorically refused to inform upon anyone. This brave precedent was followed by others at later points in the hearing.

At the beginning of the morning session on Wednes-

[50]

day, Attorney Clifford O'Brien, counsel for Mr. and Mrs. Burton James of the Seattle Repertory Theater, asked permission to read a statement. I discovered later that this was a request to cross-examine witnesses who had testified adversely about the Playhouse and its staff. When Canwell forbade O'Brien to read this request, Mrs. James rose angrily to demand that the witnesses be recalled and interrogated. She was forcibly evicted from the hearing room by officers of the State Patrol. As the hearing wore on such violent acts of eviction became more and more frequent.

Houston then called George Hewitt, a Negro from New York City. Hewitt testified that Mrs. James was a Communist whom he had met several times in Moscow, and that her assigned role was to develop pro-Soviet agitation in the American cultural field. This was the first time I had seen Hewitt, and his few moments on the stand made no deep impression. I had not the slightest premonition that this man would later testify against me.

The next witness, Howard Rushmore, was a reporter for Hearst's *New York Journal-American* who identified himself as a former Communist Party member. He charged that many prominent figures in the United States government were, or had been, Communists, naming particular persons as undercover spies for the Soviet Union. Little or no evidence was cited to support many of these defamations, and Houston did nothing to test their accuracy by cross-examining the witness.

With more show of evidence than in some other instances, Rushmore cited an "F.B.I. report" naming Alger Hiss, among others, as a former member of a "highly secret cell of the Communist Party." This cell, he said, collected "confidential information of interest to the Soviet

[51]

Government" which was transmitted to the Russian Embassy. Since I knew nothing about Hiss, the mention of his name made no impression upon me. Two weeks after Rushmore's testimony, Whittaker Chambers testified against Alger Hiss before the House Committee on Un-American Activities. This started the momentous chain of events that brought imprisonment to Hiss and fame to Richard Nixon, a zealous new member of the House committee. Since Rushmore's testimony was the first public disclosure of the charges against Hiss, Canwell in later political campaigns was able to boast that his committee had "broken" the Hiss case.

Before Rushmore left the stand, he also charged that American Communists "believe in assassination," and "would be loyal only to Russia" in event of war with the United States. "No member of the Communist Party who is a school teacher," he concluded, "can be called either an American or a teacher. He deserves the same treatment . . . as the [executed] Nazi saboteurs who came over in the submarine, or the same treatment that he would receive in Russia should he disagree with Stalin."

As I sat among the captive audience listening to the violent tone of this testimony, my original nonchalance began to change to a profound state of shock.

The first witness after Rushmore was my colleague in the Philosophy Department, Professor Herbert Phillips. He had been teaching in the summer session at Columbia University and had arrived at the hearing after a hurried trip from the airport. Being duly sworn, he asked that his testimony be postponed until he had time to consult his attorney John Caughlan. When I saw that he was being pressured to testify without benefit of counsel, I felt that I had a duty to protest. So I rose to my feet and asked, "May I say a word?"

"No . . . ," snapped the chairman. "We are not going to disrupt the hearing from the rear of the room." I was not in the rear of the room, but the remark was directed at me.

After Phillips again requested legal advice, Canwell ordered him to testify before noon or no later than two o'clock whether or not he could reach his attorney.

When he did return before the noon recess he was accompanied by Caughlan.

As Phillips mounted the stand, Caughlan asked permission to state a legal objection. He was told that no objections would be permitted. He then asked if Mr. Phillips would be allowed to state any objections.

"No, he will not," said Canwell. "We are not going to debate the issue of the legality of this Committee or its processes."

"I have a third question to ask," responded Caughlan.

"You will ask no more questions," ordered Canwell. "We are not going to go on with any ridiculous procedure here. You will either comply with the instructions of the Committee or you will be removed. Now, let's understand that for good. Are you going to comply? You are going to comply with the procedure here, or you are not going to be here."

Houston then proceeded to examine Phillips. "I haven't had time to have thorough consultation with counsel," Phillips explained, "so I'm not making my replies on advice of counsel."

When he was asked whether he had ever been a member of the Communist Party he responded inarticulately,

"For conscience—conscience sake, and political sake, I refuse to answer the question."

Phillips was then threatened with punishment for contempt of the legislature, and Mr. Caughlan again tried to speak, "May I—"

He was told to be silent. "We will hold you in contempt in a moment," snapped Canwell, "if you continue your obstinate attitude."

Another witness on Wednesday, Katherine Fogg, testified that I was a "fellow traveler," but "not a Communist." Mrs. Fogg was a person I did not recognize, and her brief testimony about me was vague. Cross-examination, if that had been possible, would have quickly exposed how shallow was her knowledge.

As I listened to the questioning of one witness after another I became more and more incensed. No attorney was allowed to present objections to questions or procedures which he regarded as violating his client's legal rights. No effort was made to discover whether any of the accused had won a reputation for integrity, loyalty, or fine scholarship. Accusatory witnesses made long and uninterrupted statements, but those under accusation were peremptorily silenced when they sought to speak in their own defence. Whenever a witness refused to act as an informer, he was threatened with a contempt citation. In a good many instances, a witness or his attorney was forcibly expelled from the hearing room by the State Patrol.

When I returned home late Wednesday afternoon I tried to tell Virginia what had been happening, but instead of giving a coherent account I broke into a violent and uncontrollable fit of weeping. Ashamed of my weakness I rushed out and mowed the lawn with savage fury. At Virginia's urging, I called my friend Dr. William

Stellwagen and secured a prescription for phenobarbital to quiet my nerves. By bedtime I was extremely tired but too much on edge to sleep without medicine. To remind myself that I must avoid an overdose, I put the medicine so high on a shelf that I would have to stand on a chair to reach it. Perhaps it is unseemly to tell these details, but I am trying to be completely candid.

On Thursday morning I went down to the Armory feeling tired and dejected. I was sick of that awful, sterile hearing room with armed guards ready to pounce upon protestors, and the shouts of dissent rising from the picket line outside the building.

The first witness was Mrs. Sarah Eldridge, a plump middle-aged woman whom I had casually known in the League against War and Fascism. Tossing metaphor after metaphor, she explained that I had turned a somersault like "the daring young man on a flying trapeze" whenever the Communist bosses gave the signal. Both in my organizational activities and in my book *No Compromise* I had been a "powerful instrument" in "softening up" the public for the spread of Communist ideas. For all practical purposes I was a Communist. "When you see a bird," she sagely remarked, "that looks like a duck, walks like a duck, and quacks like a duck, it's a duck." With similar colorful language she denounced other professors.

Mrs. Eldridge's testimony astonished me. She was the mother of Jim Eldridge, a former student of mine and a friend of long standing. When occasionally I had met her she was invariably cordial. Her opinions appeared to be liberal, and I never suspected that she would turn informer for the Committee on Un-American Activities, but her testimony against me made more plausible the damning accusation that was soon to follow.

[55]

The next witness, ex-Communist Howard F. Smith, accused a number of individuals of Communist affiliation. In the course of his testimony he used the term "nigger," whereupon George Hewitt rose suddenly to his feet and proposed "a retraction or a rejection of the remark." When Houston and Canwell concurred with this request Attorney Caughlan asked, "Mr. Chairman, is the record to be falsified?" The chairman denounced Caughlan in strong language for his interjection. "If he persists in trying to disrupt these hearings he will be removed," declared Canwell, "regardless of his—the wish of his clients to represent them. . . . Before this Committee he has no standing as an attorney or as a citizen or as a man." Caughlan was standing erect and silent as he listened to Canwell's tongue-lashing, but his whole body shook with violent emotion.

At this point O'Brien called out from the audience, "May I ask a question as counsel for a witness?"

"You may put it in writing," replied Canwell, but O'Brien persisted.

"I want to inquire," he said, "whether the Committee is presuming to instruct counsel in their duty to their clients?"

"This hearing is conducted for the Legislature, and not for the Communist Party, or their counsel" the chairman retorted, "and we will tolerate no more interference from counsel from the back of the room. Now, if that is not understood we will direct the State Patrol to remove said counsel from the hearing room."

"I bow to force," retorted O'Brien.

Some students in the audience protested, and Canwell ordered them carried out by the patrol.

As the morning wore on the tension and violence increased. Caughlan's law partner, C. T. Hatten, tried to represent Joseph Butterworth of the English Department, but when Hatten objected to a question and mentioned the right of cross-examination, Canwell instructed the State Patrol to remove him. Caughlan tried to make a remark, but he also was expelled, and the Chairman sternly declared: "Mr. Caughlan is not to return to this hearing room again while this hearing is in session. If he does I am instructing the State Patrol to put—place him under arrest."

"Mr. Chairman," remonstrated Professor Butterworth, "I am not represented by counsel." He asked that O'Brien represent him, noting that there was no opportunity to confer with his new attorney. But Houston pressed the question, "Mr. Butterworth, are you, or have you ever been a member of the Communist Party?"

"Because of conscience, and because I—this body has no right to force me to testify against myself, I refuse to answer the question."

Butterworth was ordered to step down from the stand, and the noon recess began.

I ate lunch with several friends at a nearby restaurant. As the time for the afternoon session approached, we walked back to the Armory Building and into the main lobby. Suddenly I felt an arm on my shoulder and turned to confront one of the committee's staff. He said, "Mr. Canwell wants to see you in his office."

As I walked toward the office with a feeling of uneasiness, I remembered that Ed Henry had instructed me not to confer with Canwell or any of his associates unless accompanied by counsel or a friendly witness. I resolved to follow these instructions.

The office seemed rather crowded. Mr. Canwell began, "We would like to ask you some questions."

"I am sorry, Mr. Canwell," I said, "but I have been

instructed by my attorney not to answer questions in his absence."

"Don't be alarmed," replied Canwell. "We only want to make a few inquiries."

"I shall follow my attorney's instructions and leave the room," I said as I headed for the door.

"Then ask Ed Henry to come to the office and talk with us," Canwell called after me as I was leaving.

To the best of my memory this was all that was said. Later I searched my mind to recall whether George Hewitt was in the room. I suppose he must have been, but, if he was, the fact made no impression on me. He was a stranger, and his presence meant nothing to me.

Since this brief interview became the subject of hot dispute, I shall quote from a memorandum prepared four days after the incident by Ed Henry's law partner, Paul Coughlin (not related to John Caughlan, who had been so severely rebuked by Canwell). After Hewitt had made his sensational attack upon me, Henry and Coughlin confronted the committee in private, shortly before two o'clock on Friday, and a discussion of my alleged confrontation with Hewitt ensued. Coughlin reported what transpired in his memorandum: "I established to my own satisfaction by questioning Canwell and Houston that the claim . . . that Rader had recognized Hewitt and had told him that he would not talk to him was entirely false. Rader had at first no recollection of any incident where this sort of thing could by any possibility have occurred, but after talking to Ed Henry . . . I surmised that the claim arose out of an incident that Rader described to me on the evening of Thursday, July 22nd." Coughlin then related the occurrences in Canwell's office that I have described above. "When I was talking to the Committee," he continued, "I learned from Canwell and Houston that besides themselves Hewitt was in the room sitting on a low settee which would have placed him considerably below the others and in a position where one might very well not have seen him when coming into the room. But more important I found by asking Mr. Canwell first about the incident that he gave a version almost exactly like that of Rader, indicating that the conversation turned upon the propriety of having a conversation in the absence of the attorney and also evidencing, I thought, some slight shame over the incident in which they had tricked Mr. Rader into coming into the room in the absence of Mr. Henry."

Later there were several strange versions of the incident. Houston and Hewitt both claimed that I recognized Hewitt upon entering Canwell's office, whereupon an expression of shock came over my face and I was intent only upon escaping. A similar story was contained in the official report of the committee to the Washington State Legislature and repeated by District Attorney Samuel J. Foley at the Hewitt extradition hearing in New York City. Another version was told by reporter Fred Niendorff in the *Seattle Post-Intelligencer* on July 23. According to Niendorff, Hewitt's testimony against me occurred as the result of a "dramatic encounter" in the corridor of the Armory a short time before Hewitt was to go on the stand. The look of consternation on my face, Niendorff's readers were told, confirmed Hewitt's memory of my Communist past. All of these versions were intended to point to my "guilt." We must now return to the narrative of what was happening Thursday afternoon, July 22.

After my interview with Canwell in his office, I walked up the stairs to the hearing room. I found that it was already crowded and that Ed Henry was in the audience. I told him what had happened, and he went down to the office.

I sat in the space reserved for witnesses and waited. Henry, looking very worried, returned in about half an hour. He drew me out into the hall just as the afternoon hearing was getting under way.

"Something very surprising has happened," he said. "A Negro named Hewitt is going to testify that he was your teacher in a secret Communist school back in New York State. Melvin, I advise you to tell me the truth."

"The charge is false," I said.

"All right, let's return and listen to the testimony," he replied.

We went back to our seats. Several witnesses testified briefly, and then George Hewitt was called to the stand. I looked at him closely. He was a stocky, light-complexioned Negro about my own age, with a high-domed forehead and heavy eyebrows. His attire—a cream-colored suit, white shirt, and loud striped necktie—was rather sporty.

He testified that he had been a member of the Communist Party from 1927 to 1944, using the aliases "Edward Jackson," "George James," and "Timothy Holmes." High in the counsels of the Party, he had been a member of the national committee, an editor of the newspaper *Negro Liberator*, a teacher in the Workers' School in New York City, and a delegate to the Lenin School in Moscow, where he met Stalin himself. After his return to the United States in 1935 he became an educational director for the Party.

"In the State of New York, in the year 1938 and '39," he explained, "there was for the first time a practical attempt to carry out the decisions of a conference that we had in Moscow. . . . It was the first secret school of professionals ever held in this country. It had about seventy students. . . ."

"Now where was this school held?" asked Houston.

"Up near Kingston, New York, on Briehl's Farm."

Hewitt then explained that the students were professors from American universities, that they had been carefully selected and screened by the national committee of the Party, and that he had taught at the school and was conversant with the students.

When asked whether there was anyone in Seattle who had attended the school he mentioned Professor Ralph Gundlach and me. There was no "shadow of a doubt" about the identification, and neither Gundlach nor I, he declared, could have attended that school without being a member of the Party and selected by the national committee.

"Now you are positive that that is the Melvin Rader you have seen here in this room?"

"Yes, sir. A little thinner."

"And that you met face to face less than an hour ago."

"Yes, sir."

"Now what year was this school held?"

"That was in the—about the year '39—'38 and '39."

" '38 and '39."

"Yes, sir."

" '38 and '39. How long was the course?"

"It was supposed to be a course of a month and a half. . . . Six weeks intensive study of Marxism and Leninism for the professional personnel."

He went on to say that the students in the school had been instructed in "the ethics of Stalin and the ethics of

Soviet America for the destruction of our great country. . . . That is, the bloody overthrow of this—of the United States Government."

Houston then asked, "Are there members who keep their membership secret even from other Communist members?"

"Oh, definitely."

". . . Would it become possible," Houston asked, "for a member of the Communist Party to be a teacher at the University of Washington, and that fact not even be known to other Communist teachers?"

"Very definitely so," replied Hewitt. "Very definitely so."

"Is that—would that be an unusual case?"

"No. There are several such cases."

This supersecret member, Hewitt explained, would be subject to very strict discipline and have "a function completely separate" from the ordinary Communist.

So this was the charge! I was a secret Party member intensively trained for the higher echelons, and the training school was at Briehl's Farm in New York State.

I was tired and emotionally shaken when the hearing recessed for the day. Ed Henry and I walked down the hall and talked about what should be done. "I don't know you very well," Henry said to me. "I would feel better if you would let Paul handle this matter." Since his partner Paul Coughlin had been my roommate in college and was an intimate friend, I welcomed the suggestion. We drove out to Paul's home on a hill overlooking Puget Sound. There his wife Margaret served dinner, and we talked about how to bring a perjurer to justice.

Before bidding us good-bye for the evening, Ed Henry related what had happened during the afternoon, mentioning that he had arranged with Houston for Paul to cross-examine Hewitt the next day, Friday, at noon. In preparation for this cross-examination, it would be necessary to get the facts straight. Since Hewitt had testified that I had attended the Briehl's Farm school nine or ten years before, I began to rack my memory to reconstruct exactly what I had been doing in those years. As the evening wore on there were long telephone conversations with Virginia, and, thanks to her remarkable memory, we were able to piece together a fairly detailed account of my activities in the summers of 1938 and 1939. Then Paul telephoned long distance to one of the deputy prosecutors, Max Nicolai, who was vacationing at a Puget Sound resort, Birch Bay. He was a former student and a friend of mine, and, knowing my character, he had no doubt that Hewitt's testimony was false. Both he and Paul then called the prosecuting attorney of King County, Lloyd Shorett, who promised to investigate the next day.

It was long past midnight when I returned home. Virginia had gone to bed but was still awake. She wanted to know the details of Hewitt's testimony which I had sketched to her only briefly. I related the full story, and she sat bolt upright in amazement. "No!" she said. "Not really!"

I undressed and went to bed but could not sleep. Turning on the light, I tried to lose myself in a mystery novel, but it seemed too remote and unreal. After awhile I managed to sleep fitfully. That night Virginia slept no better than I.

6

Moment

of

Crisis

WHEN we awoke the next morning Hewitt's story was already top news on the radio and in the papers. The situation was very serious—I would be disgraced and my career would be ruined if he succeeded in convincing the public and the regents of the university. My dismissal from the faculty would bring great hardship not only to myself but to Virginia and the children. On the other hand, if we could expose Hewitt as a liar and secure his arrest and conviction, we would deal a near-mortal blow to this infamous committee and the political ambitions of its members. I began to realize that we were playing for big stakes.

Early Friday morning I sat at the breakfast table watching the squirrels in their morning acrobatics. Virginia soon joined me, and together we drafted a statement to give to the newsmen. Then I went to the telephone and called the president of the university and Dean Edwin

Guthrie, his principal assistant, telling them that I expected to be put on the stand and that I would like them to be present. Later I was disappointed when neither appeared at the hearing.

Arriving at the Armory a little early, I found a number of inquisitive newsmen. We retired to a press room where I read them the statement that Virginia and I had prepared: "I have never been, and I am not now, a member of the Communist Party of the United States of America, nor of any other Communist Party at any time or in any place. I have always been, and am now, a liberal and a believer in democracy. I have reached all my decisions independently, as an individual, and never at the behest, the instruction, or the dictation of the Communist Party or any Communist Front or any other party or organization. Whenever I have favored any cause, such as that of Loyalist Spain, or joined or participated in any organization, such as the American League against War and Fascism, my decision has been for democratic, humanitarian, and non-Communist reasons. While reserving all my constitutional rights, I shall testify to all this and more before the Canwell Committee or any court of law. I shall answer all questions addressed to me to the best of my knowledge and belief, and I shall evade none." This declaration was never published. The newsmen evidently preferred to reproduce my testimony on the stand rather than quote from a prepared statement. Nevertheless, the statement helped to steady my resolve.

After talking to the newsmen I took my reserved seat toward the front of the hearing room. As the session was about to begin Attorney O'Brien jumped up and hastily passed out mimeographed sheets to reporters and others in the audience. Canwell sharply reprimanded him, but quite a number of copies had already been distributed. The copy handed to me reproduced a two-page letter that O'Brien had sent by registered mail to Prosecutor Shorett, with carbon copies to Chairman Canwell and the state attorney-general. The letter declared: "Both Mrs. James and Dr. Gundlach are prepared to swear to complaints or to warrants of arrest for perjury against the witness George Hewitt. . . . If it would be possible for you immediately to send a representative of your office or yourself to go to the 146th Field Artillery to investigate these plain perjuries of the witness Hewitt, both Mrs. James and Dr. Gundlach will be most happy to cooperate. . . ." It is noteworthy that the official transcript of the hearing omits any reference to this incident.

In the meantime, Paul Coughlin, as my attorney, went to the County-City Building to see Shorett. True to his promise of the night before, the prosecutor dispatched his chief deputy, Major Herbert H. Davis, formerly of Army Intelligence, to cross-examine Hewitt. Paul also arranged for a court reporter to accompany them and make a record of the cross-examination. The committee was already in session and Hewitt was back on the stand when Major Davis, Paul, and the reporter arrived at the Armory shortly before twelve. They were forced to await the noon recess before approaching the committee.

On the stand, Hewitt told in detail about his experiences at the Lenin School in Moscow, where he and others were allegedly trained in infiltration and sabotage, the use of secret codes, the making of hand grenades, and the handling of firearms. "I had the occasion to meet Mr. Stalin four different times," Hewitt declared. "One was at . . . a regular dinner in the Kremlin with the President Kallinen, Kagonovitch . . . Molotov. There were many luminaries. . . ." At one of the meetings, Hewitt said, he personally delivered to Stalin a letter of grievances against the "corrupt leadership" of the American Communist Party. Subsequently Hewitt taught political economy and physical education in the Lenin School. He also "worked very closely with . . . Red Army officials."

Asked about seeing Mrs. James in Russia, Hewitt replied that she was associated with the Meyerhold Theater, one of the most popular cultural institutions in Moscow. "I was very intimate with the aides of Mr. Meyerhold," he said, adding that he discussed Mrs. James and other Americans with the directors of the theater.

"You're a liar!" shouted Burton James from the audience, and O'Brien cried out, "Perjurer!" "Take him out," the chairman ordered, and O'Brien was ejected.

Hewitt then declared that the charge of perjury did not affect him "one iota," remarking that he had similarly been charged in the Santo trial in New York.

He spoke of his years of teaching in "secret and professional schools" in the United States. Houston asked him about the school at Briehl's Farm near Kingston: "Now you testified that two Seattle people were there."

"Yes, sir," replied Hewitt.

"You're positive of this? I say, you are positive of this?"

"Definitely."

"No question or doubt?"

"No, sir."

Hewitt described Briehl's Farm school and others of this type. Every effort was made, he explained, to hide the identity of the students. "We had to be careful of the people we selected . . . ," he said. "They were instructed how . . . to lie, how to use every ruse . . . to smear anyone that would divulge or disclose their identity." The students were instructed in the "illegal tactics" approved by Lenin. "Under the mere term illegal," Hewitt explained, "both Communists and Fascists include murder, assassination, theft, bombings, wrecking of industrial plants, machinery, and many other outrages, which under American standards of law and morals are classified as crimes."

Houston asked, "Now, why did you get out of the Communist Party?"

"I got out of the Communist Party, my dear Mr. Houston," began Hewitt, "a very a—the—us—excuse me." His words tumbled after one another in unintelligible confusion. He used the word "fantasy" entirely out of context and referred to his old black mother. I watched and listened very closely, wondering if the man was mad. Putting the best face he could on this gibberish, Houston remarked, "I realize this is a matter of great emotion to you."

After recovering enough to continue, Hewitt accused the Communists of persecuting and trying to kill him. The Party bigwigs had tried to send him into areas infested by the Ku Klux Klan in the hope that he would be murdered. Later, when he was no longer a Party member, Communists had mercilessly harassed him and his family. "When my last baby was born," he said, "they used a time when my wife would nurse the little child and pull out the fuse [*sic*]. . . . They ripped my baby carriage. They attempted to tell people in the neighborhood not to play handball with me. . . . They went to my employers and told them that I was a drunkard, and I never drank in my life. The Russians tried to get me to taste that vile thing called Vodka but I saw what it did to Nazula, the South African Secretary, who drank a little bit of it. They

[68]

picked him up in the snow dead the following morning. . . ."

Houston asked, "Is it not a common practice among the Communist Party to file all kinds of harassing lawsuits, perjury charges against witnesses that testify against them?"

"Yes, sir. . . . To give the underworld, the gangster underworld, the go-ahead signal. . . ."

"If it runs true to pattern, before this hearing's over we'll have that kind of stuff here, will we?"

"They will attempt—yes, without a question of doubt—"

"And that definitely is Communist Party line?"

"It is."

As I listened to Hewitt's interminable testimony, I seemed to be sinking down and down through a bottomless ocean of fatigue. I had slept badly the whole week and scarcely at all the night before. Just to keep my eyes and ears open was supremely difficult. When I managed to do so I noticed that Investigator Stith, who was standing some distance away, had his eyes riveted upon me. It crossed my mind that he had been assigned the task of breaking down my morale with his relentless cold stare, and this fancy held me like a vise. If their strategy was to make me "break," they were close to succeeding.

When Hewitt stepped down from the stand, Chairman Canwell announced: "We will be in recess until two o'clock this afternoon."

I met Paul Coughlin in the hall. "Don't leave," he said. "We are trying to arrange a confrontation with Hewitt. You will be questioned along with him."

So instead of going to lunch I stayed in the building. I got some chocolate bars and Coca Cola out of a vending machine, and then I roamed aimlessly around the halls with nothing to do. The time stretched on and on, and nothing happened. Feeling jittery, I decided to jot down what I might be called upon to testify. I squatted on the floor in the hall, took some paper from my pocket, and began to write down the things I had been doing in 1938 and 1939. I was still at work when people began to drift back into the hearing room, so I took my seat and continued to scribble.

Meanwhile Coughlin and Henry had been trying to reach Hewitt in order to cross-examine him. During the brief morning recess Henry asked Houston if Prosecuting Attorney Shorett or one of his deputies could be present during the questioning. Houston snapped back, "You can't use any of those Communist tactics on my witnesses!" Henry reminded him that pressure would probably be put upon Shorett to file a perjury charge, and that it was only fair to the prosecutor to allow him to hear both sides and to question Hewitt before deciding whether to file the charge. Finally Houston said he would consider the matter and take it up with the committee.

During the long noon recess Henry again tried to arrange for the confrontation. He went into the office and talked with Houston and some members of the committee. Although the understanding had been that the questioning would occur during this noon recess, Henry was put off and told to return at 1:30. At the appointed time, Davis substituting for Henry appeared and talked to Houston and the committee members. He demanded the right, as deputy prosecutor, to question Hewitt. He was told that the committee would consult its attorney, Ford Elvidge, and would give its answer at 5:30 that afternoon. Then Henry and Coughlin were also admitted to the committee meeting for a brief discussion, but nothing very important transpired.

Chairman Canwell gaveled the afternoon session to order at about 2:15. The first witness was Lane Summers, an attorney whose son Thane, as I have explained, was killed in Spain fighting with the Abraham Lincoln Brigade. The father named me and several other professors as the corrupters of his son, charging that we had converted him to Communism and were ultimately responsible for his death. This accusation cut me to the quick, for I had been very fond of Thane.

Five additional witnesses, some friendly and others unfriendly, testified one after another.

My fatigue returned in deeper waves. When I shook myself awake I noticed that Stith was continuing his unrelenting stare. Suddenly my name was called, and my heart began to pound. This was it! I walked to the witness stand, raised my hand to be sworn, and sat down. Ed Henry took his seat by my side.

After a few preliminaries Houston asked, "Are you or have you ever been a member of the Communist Party?"

With my heart still pounding, I started to draw forth the statement that Virginia and I had prepared for the newsmen. "I think I can answer the question best if I can read a statement," I began. Then I had enough presence of mind to realize that a written statement would seem artificial. "I will answer the question *No*," I said, pocketing the statement. "I have never been a member of the Communist Party, and I am not now a member of the Communist Party, and I shall be glad to elaborate that answer any time."

Houston then asked me a series of questions about my affiliations and activities during the Depression and the

[71]

Spanish Civil War. The interrogation became a sparring match in which he sought to expose me as subversive and I countered with the truth. His questions were very specific. For example, he asked, "On Sunday evening April 7, 1935, in the Labor Temple in the City of Seattle, did you speak for an hour and ten minutes on the Soviet Union at a meeting of the American League Against War and Fascism?"

"Well sir, you have stated the question in such very definite and such very precise terms," I said, "that I don't see how I could answer that question 'Yes' or 'No' without perjuring myself. . . . I can't remember precisely. That's quite a time ago. It may well have been under those auspices, it may well have been on that exact day, and it may well have been that precise length of time."

"Now I'll ask you if you spoke to a political rally of the Communist Party under the auspices of the Washington Commonwealth Federation, in a fraction meeting in the Senator Auditorium, September 18th, 1939."

"I'm very certain I did not do that, sir."

"You did not?"

"I did not do that, sir, unless the meeting was so completely and utterly disguised that I, as a person who is not a Communist, and who has never been a Communist, was totally unable to recognize the nature of the meeting."

"Now on February the 9th, 1939, did you sponsor a meeting in the Moore Hotel for the purpose of raising money for the Communist Government of Spain in exile?"

"May I say, Mr. Houston, that I never interpreted any statement that I have ever made in all my life as defense or advocacy of any Communist government in Spain or elsewhere. Again you are asking me a question about a particular date. Now these are events that took place many years ago, and I, gentlemen, do not have a perfect memory and I doubt if, indeed, I could act as if I did, without telling untruth here, which I don't intend to do. I will say this, that I have spoken from time to time in favor of Loyalist Spain, interpreting 'Loyalist Spain' as not a Communist government."

"Now, I will ask you if you participated on August 23rd, 1941, in an Anti-Fascist Mass meeting in the Bothell High School at 8:00 P.M.?"

"Well, sir, I just can't answer that question in the sense that I know that it is or is not the case. I can't remember."

When questions of this type persisted Canwell interposed, "The witness is well within what is reasonable in saying that he cannot remember a specific hour or a date ten years ago."

"Thank you, Mr. Canwell," I replied.

"Well," asked Mr. Houston, "have you followed the Communist Party line, Doctor?"

"I have never been and I am not now a follower of the Communist Party line," I responded. "I have reached all my decisions independently, as an individual, and never at the behest or the instruction or the dictation of the Communist Party or any Communist front organization or any other party or organization."

"After the Hitler-Stalin Pact in September 1939, did you label the war an imperialistic war?"

"I think you have the date of that pact slightly wrong."

"Now your memory is much better there. I was testing you. The pact was in August 1939, wasn't it?"

"It was about then."

"I just wanted to test your memory. It isn't so bad on some things, is it, Doctor?"

"Yes, but you were referring then to a very, very famous historical event. Almost anybody who has any interest in history would make a real effort to remember it, sir."

"Well, can you answer the question?"

"All right. Would you repeat the question, because I want to be sure of the correct terms."

"After the Hitler-Stalin Pact, did you label the ensuing war an imperialistic war?"

"I think it will take two or three sentences to answer that question. May I have those sentences?"

"Yes," replied Houston, but Canwell interposed, "I think it will be easy to answer whether you did or not, and then I think you may enlarge upon that."

"I don't think," I replied, "that I ever did in an unqualified way."

"You can enlarge on that if you want to," Houston remarked.

"All right, thank you. I want to point out that this was a period in which my book *No Compromise* was before the public. . . . Now I wrote a preface for British readers to that book, a preface that never appeared in the American edition. That preface was sent by trans-Atlantic air mail to London, and it appears in the English copy. . . . In that preface, written sometime during September 1939, I strongly expressed my sympathies, my solidarity, and my loyalty, not only to American democracy but to the whole concept of democracy internationally and specifically to France and England. I don't know whether that answers your questions, sir. Do you want any more elaboration?"

"No, you wanted to elaborate."

During this period of interrogation I had largely shaken off my fear and fatigue. Drawing upon some unsuspected reserve of energy I found myself fresh and alert. I began to suspect that Houston was more tired than I.

"Have you ever been aware of Communist activity on the campus?" he asked.

"Well, sir," I replied, "my knowledge of such activity is just what any ordinary faculty person's knowledge is. I could engage in speculation, I have heard rumors, but I take it this is a fact-finding committee and you are not interested in my speculations."

When Houston demanded a definite answer, I recalled that some handbills had been passed out by the Young Communist League or some such organization.

Houston turned to the crucial question: "Well, now, you heard the testimony yesterday afternoon of the witness George Hewitt. I'll ask you, did you ever attend a school at Briehl Farm near Kingston, New York?"

"Emphatically not, sir," I replied.

"Other than 'not' would you mind using the word 'no'?"

"No."

"I'll ask you if you attended a Communist Party School anywhere in the summer of 1938, or the summer of 1939?"

"No."

"Where were you in the summer of 1938," Houston demanded.

"I'll try to answer that as fully as I can," I said, glancing down at the notes I had prepared during the noon recess.

"What are the notes that you are reading?" asked Houston. I explained that I had made these notes in the hall during the recess, and that I wrote them out because I wanted to be accurate about a very serious accusation involving two whole summers a long time ago.

When Houston continued to object to the notes, I replied, "I'm swearing to everything I say under oath." The chairman then ruled that I could refer to the notes if I so desired.

In 1938, I explained, I taught in the first half of the summer session and shortly thereafter went with my family to Canyon Creek Lodge near Granite Falls for a six weeks' vacation. I also recalled being in Seattle during September. "I remember this clearly," I declared. "It was the time of the Munich crisis, and I stayed very close to my radio."

"Now, Doctor, let's get to the point," said Houston. "We're talking about '38 and the Munich period was in '39." It was Houston who was wrong about the date, and not I. There was a ripple of laughter that ran through the audience when he still insisted on the wrong date and when, to his embarrassment, I continued to correct him.

When I again referred to my notes, Canwell urged me to dispense with them.

"Well, sir, I could certainly make the attempt," I replied. "I'm afraid if I did I might not be as accurate, and I would like to be accurate."

"I'll let you use your judgment," Canwell said.

I bent over and conferred with Ed Henry. He advised me to continue to use my notes, and this I did. Testifying about the summer of 1939, I recalled that I again taught at the university during the first half of the summer term; that I was in Seattle when the first copies of my new book, *No Compromise*, reached the bookstores early in August; and that I remained in Seattle or the near vicinity until the outbreak of the war.

Canwell asked me to be brief. "Yes, surely," I said. "I will be as brief as I can and be fair to myself, sir." After again conferring with Henry, I requested permission to

[76]

state the only time I had ever been in New York. It was, I explained, for a period of about ten days in the summer of 1945 after I had completed a year of teaching at the University of Chicago. "I went," I said, "to see my son, Gordon Rader, who was in New York at that time, and also to see New York."

Houston contended that I could have been in New York during the period when I was "allegedly . . . at this Canyon Creek Lodge."

"But not allegedly, sir," I replied. "I feel quite confident about it."

"Well, if you wanted to go to New York instead of Canyon Creek Lodge you could have been there, couldn't you?"

"No sir, I did not want to go to New York, I was not in New York, there are people who know where I was."

There was a similar exchange about 1939.

I was then asked whether I had ever been solicited for membership in the Communist Party by a member of the faculty.

"I'm not absolutely certain," I replied. "I thought I had. I went to the person that I thought had solicited me, and asked him. He said he was confident he had not."

I was then asked whether I had ever been solicited a second time. I mentioned that I had been approached by Bob Roberts, a well-known professional organizer for the Communist Party. Since he had been an open Party member, I was exposing no one by this answer.

Houston continued to press me for the name of the faculty member who had denied that he had ever asked me to join the Party. At this point I was in a delicate situation. I had told the press that I would answer every question and I intended to keep my word. Also if I refused to answer I could be threatened with contempt and summarily dismissed from the stand. This, I felt, would be a victory for the Committee and would weaken the effect of my testimony.

"Well, sir, I hope I can't remember any individual," I said. "I don't like a bit to inform. . . . I don't intend to allow you to cite me for contempt. I told the members of the press sometime this morning that I would evade no question . . . and that is the way I am proceeding."

I paused and felt the rising tenseness in the crowd. The room was absolutely still as they waited to see if I would break down and join the ranks of informers.

"Therefore, since you force me," I resumed, "I am going to answer that question to the very best of my knowledge and ability. I thought, sir, until it was denied by the man I am about to name, that it was Sophus Keith Winther."

I had exposed no one, since Winther himself had testified similarly on the stand and had identified himself as a former Communist. The name broke the tension and frustrated Houston's drive to uncover a new suspect.

Houston returned to the attack: "Do you believe in the form of government that exists in the United States, Dr. Winther—I mean, Dr. Rader?"

"I certainly believe, sir, in the Constitution of the United States and the Bill of Rights, and the government set up under that Constitution, as it would be interpreted, for example, by the Supreme Court."

"Do you believe in the capitalist form of government as it exists in the United States of America today?"

"Not in every single feature of it, sir."

"What features would you change?"

"I would change those features that . . . tend to bring

about great economic catastrophes, namely great depressions, and that, in consequence of this, threaten the very structure of our democracy itself."

"How would you change the system?"

"One thing I would be thoroughly for and anxious to do, and I think it is very needful, and that is to change our system of society, particularly in the City of Seattle at the present time, in the direction of a more complete obedience in spirit and letter to the Bill of Rights."

After a few more questions Chairman Canwell asked, "I wonder, Mr. Houston, how long you expect this to go on, or shall we have a recess?"

"I'm presently through," Houston responded. "I'm very weary—I'll just ask you one thing further. Would you be willing to work with our investigators, Doctor, in definitely and positively ascertaining with documentary evidence where you were in 1938 and '39, which you don't remember?"

"Mr. Houston," I replied, "I would be very glad to work with the Prosecuting Attorney of King County or any of his deputies or governmental officials of the State of Washington that my counsel would approve."

"Counsel," Houston said addressing Henry, "can we expect any cooperation out of Dr. Rader?"

"Well, I think he has answered your question already," Henry replied.

"Mr. Chairman," Houston said, "I would like to point out for the record's sake that we attempted to cooperate with Mr. Rader during the course of the investigation. He refused. We subpoenaed him to the office—he refused to talk. Yesterday we asked him, prior to the testimony of the witness, to sit down with the witness and confront the witness. He refused. . . ."

I started to protest but I was not allowed to finish. Then Henry asked to put into the record a statement counter to Houston's remark. "I don't want to be thrown out of here but I—" he began.

"If you wish to cooperate with us," replied Canwell, "or to advise your client to cooperate with us in getting information helpful to his side of the question, we most certainly will do it; but I don't think we will carry this discussion any further."

After a few more words I was excused from the stand.

There was one more witness, a professor who denied the charge that he had been a member of the Communist Party, but I was too tired and excited to listen to him. Then Canwell announced, "We will now release all people under subpoena and adjourn."

I walked out into the hall to confront Hewitt in the presence of Major Davis, expecting the cross-examination to begin. This would be the most crucial test of all.

Paul Coughlin was waiting for me. "I have news for you," he said. "They have rushed Hewitt down to the airport and spirited him out of the state."

7

Summer
Vacation

HEWITT had testified vaguely that the period of training
at Briehl's Farm was in 1938 or 1939, but eventually he
fixed upon the summer of 1938 as the crucial date. Virginia and I, month after month, ransacked our memories
to recall every slightest detail of that summer. My fate
and Hewitt's fate—perhaps even the fate of Canwell and
his committee—would depend upon our ability to remember and prove what had happened during this period. If
the incidents that I shall recount appear insignificant, the
reader must bear with me, for these were the things we
remembered and were intent upon proving. They were
thus the very heart of the matter.

As the regular university term neared a close in June of
1938, Virginia and I decided to take a vacation. I was
scheduled to teach during the first session of summer
school, but I would be free from July 20 until early
September. Some friends recommended Canyon Creek

Lodge, a resort near Granite Falls, about fifty miles northeast of Seattle in the foothillls of the Cascade Mountains. We decided to explore the area and if it should seem attractive to make a reservation for later in the summer.

We arranged to leave our baby, Miriam, with Virginia's sister and brother-in-law, Louisa and George Petterson, who were visiting us from Montana, and we sent my ten-year-old-boy, Gordon, who had been in our custody throughout the school year, to spend the summer with his mother's parents in Waterville, a country town on the eastern side of the Cascades.

Since we did not own a car, we took a bus from Seattle on the morning of June 11, planning to reach the lodge in the afternoon. But we made a mistake at a transfer point and found ourselves stranded in the village of Arlington, unable to reach our destination before nightfall, so we rented a room in a small hotel facing the town square, a small park area with grass, flowers, and trees. After breakfast the next morning we again caught the bus, this time making the right transfer and arriving at the little town of Granite Falls, four miles from the lodge, in the early afternoon. Although it was a warm day, we walked the entire remaining distance, strolling leisurely and resting in the shade from time to time. About a mile from the town, we made a brief side excursion to look at the impressive waterfalls and then trudged three miles farther to the resort.

We must have been an odd-looking couple when, hot and bedraggled, we wandered into the lodge. Ida Kirby, the caretaker, was so struck by our appearance that, when questioned by investigators ten years later, she included in her affidavit a vivid picture of how we looked: "Sometime . . . when we were having our hottest weather, a tall, slender, seedy looking man, and a woman, slightly shorter than himself, walked all the way from Granite Falls out to the Canyon Creek Lodge looking for a place to stay. They both were more or less unkept [*sic*] in their appearance, and I distinctly remember that they did not impress me as being a University professor and his wife, which they said they were. As I remember the gentleman's wife, she didn't come much more than to his shoulder in height, if that much. The one thing I do remember about her and the one thing discussed by myself, Mrs. Mueller and Mrs. Mueller's niece, Lucille, was the fact that it seemed strange that they would walk from Granite Falls to the Lodge during the heat of the day at a time when this lady was pregnant. They came without baggage. . . ."

Mrs. Quincy Mueller, the owner of the lodge, was a gracious host and made us feel welcome. She explained that the original lodge, a rustic building in a wooded setting, had burned down during the preceding February, and the new lodge, situated near the main road and less charming in appearance, had been opened for business not long before we arrived. When we asked for accommodations, she had nothing ready so early in the season except a small cabin which she used occasionally for hired help and which was not well furnished. We gladly rented the cabin, a plain little shelter close to the lodge, and spent the weekend enjoying the excellent meals and exploring the vicinity.

Most of the cabins, we discovered, were clustered not far from the lodge, but we found a single cottage named the "Graydoor" beyond a gently rolling golf course at the edge of Canyon Creek. This was exactly what we wanted. Its isolated location would give us privacy for living and quiet for my writing, and its rustic appearance, with natural timbers and large stone chimney and fireplace, captivated us. After taking several walks through the woods, we were also delighted with the vicinity. No very high peaks were in sight, but the country was fairly rugged and lush with flowers, shrubs, and trees. So we engaged the "Graydoor" cottage for the entire month of August. At the end of our weekend stay, Mrs. Mueller arranged to have us driven by car to catch our bus at Granite Falls, and we rode back to Seattle happy with the prospect of returning later in the summer.

When the time for our vacation approached, our friends, Angelo and Virginia Pellegrini, kindly volunteered to drive us up to Canyon Creek. On the first of August we made ready and packed. The car was heavily loaded, with the three of us and our baggage along with Pelly, Virginia, and their little girl, Angela, a year and a half older than our baby. When we arrived at Canyon Creek in the late afternoon, we found the "Graydoor" ready. After signing the register in the lodge, we prepared dinner for all of us in the cabin, and after dinner the Pellegrinis wished us a happy vacation and started homeward.

During the evening and night of that day certain events occurred in Seattle that fixed our departure indelibly in the memory of my mother-in-law, Mrs. Albert Baker, a semi-invalid suffering from arthritis. She had been visiting in our home, and when we prepared to go we left our key in her charge, with the understanding that she and Louisa would use the house at their convenience. After our departure, noticing that the geraniums in our windowboxes were drooping, she got out the hose and watered the flowers. That night, since Louisa and George were away, she slept in our bedroom alone. Unfortunately she had got damp and chilled while watering the flowers and this brought on a terrible attack of arthritis. Thinking that she might be dying, she screamed aloud in the dead of night in an attempt to arouse the neighbors with her calls for help, but to no avail. When the attack subsided the next morning, she managed to crawl out of bed, dress, and travel back by streetcar and ferry to her home near Bremerton, across Puget Sound from Seattle. The crisis and all the events connected with it were unforgettable, and ten years later she was ready to testify under oath, if need be, that she remembered the date and circumstances of our departure most vividly.

At Canyon Creek things worked out nicely for us. Miriam, an eighteen-month-old baby, had a big play area, and even when we kept her penned she enjoyed using cans of baby food as blocks to pile up, knock down, and toss around. I found the cabin a quiet place to work, and we enjoyed seclusion except on weekends, when there was a great influx of golfers and fishermen. The weather was sunny but seldom too hot. We spent many hours sleeping, sunbathing, or strolling through the woods. Mr. Mueller, who ran a butcher shop in Granite Falls, brought us groceries from the town; Ida Kirby, the good-natured caretaker, helped carry the food to the cabin; and Frank Ketchum, a lad employed by Mrs. Mueller, kept us well supplied with logs for our fireplace and kindling and sticks for our cookstove.

As a special treat, we occasionally ate a delicious dinner at the lodge, where Mrs. Mueller, who had a great gift for hospitality, always made us feel welcome. The lodge itself was a pleasant place to visit—on cooler evenings there was a cheerful fire burning in the huge fireplace, and the main room was attractively decorated with pictures of the old lodge building and with Indian relics and other interesting objects which Mrs. Mueller had managed to save from the fire. She sometimes talked nostalgically about the charm of the old building, and soon after our arrival she walked with Virginia down to survey the ruins, an area covered mainly by blackened rubble and ashes.

Our enjoyment was marred by two mishaps. During the early period of our stay, Virginia began to suffer from toothache, and we decided to arrange an appointment with Dr. Raymond Loy, a young dentist who came into the area two days a week to take care of the dental needs of the small population. I went with Virginia to Granite Falls and was present in the dentist's office when she was treated. The tooth, it turned out, was ulcerated and had to be pulled. It was a very difficult extraction, and with insufficient equipment for a proper anesthetic Dr. Loy pounded and chiseled for over an hour. Virginia not only suffered immediate shock but her jaw swelled badly, and she felt intense pain for several days. The experience was unforgettable.

Then on August 14, while clambering over some rocks, I dropped and broke my only pair of glasses. Since I had not been fitted with new lenses for some time, I decided to make an appointment with an oculist rather than reorder lenses from the old prescription. I telephoned to Dr. Carl Jensen in Seattle for an appointment, and early on the morning of August 15 set off by bus to the city, where Dr. Jensen tested my eyes and wrote out a prescription for new lenses. I took the prescription to an optical company and arranged to have my new glasses mailed to me at Canyon Creek Lodge.

I also telephoned Lucile Newman, Virginia's cousin,

and told her about Virginia's tooth extraction and my mishap. Lucile asked me if Virginia planned to attend the wedding of their mutual cousin, Jean Simpson, on August 17, but I explained that Virginia, still uncomfortable from her tooth extraction, was loath to interrupt our vacation. I also took a streetcar out to our Seattle home to pick up some articles we needed, and there I saw Louisa and George. Whether I stayed overnight or traveled back to Canyon Creek late that day, I cannot remember.

When we reached the end of our rental month, Ida Kirby, who had volunteered to drive us to Seattle, could not be spared at the lodge until after the rush of the Labor Day weekend, when many holiday guests were expected. So we stayed on in the "Graydoor" until the rush was over. Then we packed up the playpen, the baby, and our miscellaneous belongings, and Mrs. Kirby, in her little roustabout truck, drove us back to our Seattle home on 30th Avenue N.E.

These were the facts. To prove them would not be easy.

8

Delays

and

Frustrations

ON THE Friday evening after I testified, we expected to retire early, but the house was soon overflowing with friends. We all got joyously drunk in a spontaneous outburst of relief that the immediate crisis was over. I needed to relieve the tension, but it took more than this evening to quiet my nerves. I had worked up to a terrific pitch of excitement, and for days thereafter I felt terribly taut. Virginia, too, was near the breaking point.

We were determined to gather whatever evidence was required to indict Hewitt and to do so without delay. This meant that I would have to resign my summer teaching position in Los Angeles. Since the job was scheduled to begin in a few days, I hurried to the Western Union office and dispatched a lengthy telegram to Chancellor Dykstra of the University of California, explaining that I was in no condition to teach and that I would like him to find a substitute. Fortunately he was able to do so. I also abandoned my plan to work during the autumn at the Hoover Library in Palo Alto. It was absolutely necessary to stay at "the scene of battle" until the question of perjury was resolved.

Virginia and I conferred with Lloyd Shorett in his office as soon as the appointment could be arranged. The prosecuting attorney was a rather young man, tall and straight, with a dignified bearing. He promised to investigate and, if the evidence was compelling, to seek Hewitt's indictment and trial. To check upon my past, he enlisted the aid of the Federal Bureau of Investigation, which was willing to enter the case because an important federal witness was involved. After about two weeks he received a report from the bureau that they could find no reliable evidence that I was or had ever been a Communist Party member. Then, to eliminate the possibility of mistaken identity, he questioned Hewitt twice over long-distance telephone, and both conversations were recorded. In the first interview on July 30, Hewitt affirmed categorically that he had made no mistake in identifying me. He explained that the students at the school, while concealing their identity, talked openly of the particular place from which they had come.

"Did Rader have some assumed name there?" Shorett asked.

"All of them had assumed names."

"You didn't know him under the name of Rader?"

"No—no."

He had seen me, he said, not only at Briehl's Farm but at several places in and around New York City.

"Was Rader in any class you taught?"

"Yes," replied Hewitt. "Rader was in the one on political economy."

"Did Rader have any speech defect?" Shorett asked. Hewitt could not recall any. (I have a slight lisp.)

"Well, I'm going to tell you Rader does have a speech impediment," said Shorett. "Now if you can remember, tell me what kind of an impediment Rader has." Hewitt could not remember any impediment, but spoke of my exceptional tallness and thick glasses. (I *am* tall, but my glasses were no thicker than most.)

When Shorett sought to fix the time of the school, Hewitt said that he had gone to Briehl's Farm about the first of June in either 1938 or 1939 and had stayed about four or five weeks. At the end of the conversation, he said he might be able to fix the date by checking his records, and would telephone collect if he discovered any new evidence.

Shorett called him two days later. In this second conversation, Hewitt said the date could not have been before 1939 and might have been 1940. He told Shorett that he had determined the approximate date from a postcard received in 1940 from a former student, who had previously been with me at Briehl's Farm.

Altogether, in the two telephone interviews and Hewitt's original testimony, there was much equivocation about the date. Hence it was necessary for us to gather evidence for all three summers: 1938, 1939, and 1940.

When Virginia and I started to collect evidence, our first thought was to look through a large box of family records. Since we had recently moved into our new home, we remembered that the box had been placed on a high shelf in our bedroom closet. We had seen it many times since in that location, and neither of us had moved it. But when we went to look it had disappeared! Astonished, we questioned the children closely for any possible clue and hunted upstairs and downstairs, inside and outside the house, in every place conceivable, even the most unlikely. There was not a trace. Somebody must have entered the house and stolen the box. But who? Since the contents could have no monetary value to a stranger, we concluded that the act was not that of an ordinary thief. Apparently the intruder was searching for evidence that might incriminate me.

The loss was a dreadful shock. The box contained precious and irreplaceable family records, such as pictures of our parents when they were young, baby photographs of our children, and such personal records as birth registrations, diplomas, and our marriage certificate. Thereafter we were very careful to lock doors and to hide all our evidence in the most secret places.

The number of anonymous telephone calls we received was upsetting. I could never know, when I answered the phone, whether I was about to be denounced by some unidentified person as "a Communist rat." On two occasions a woman telephoned constantly for an hour and a half, no sooner hanging up than calling again. Even when we talked to friends, we felt constrained for fear that our line was being tapped.

The newspapers and radio had spread the news of the hearing far and wide. Wherever we went, to the drugstore or the grocery, to the university or the theater, people knew about Hewitt's charges. Many were friendly, but some were hostile. The effect upon Virginia and me was to draw us closer together. On the first Monday after the hearing we climbed up to the gallery in the Metropolitan Theater to see the road show "Oklahoma," and a number of people in the audience recognized us. We felt proud and defiant and very close to one another. In the weeks that followed we went almost everywhere together, seeking warmth and security in each other's company.

We could talk about little besides the hearing and its consequences. Even the children—Miriam eleven years old, Barbara nine, Cary seven, and David five—kept jabbering about the committee and its supporters. One of their games was to compose such rhymes as these:

> Canwell
> Go to hell.
>
> Houston
> Son of a gun.
>
> Pomeroy
> Bad boy.
>
> Niendorff
> Jump off the wharf.

But the children could not find a suitable rhyme for "Stith"—this was too hard a nut for them to crack!

Virginia and I spent many hours racking our memories. She or I would wake up excitedly in the middle of the night with the sudden recollection of something we had done in those distant summers. But it is difficult to remember and even harder to prove what you were doing eight, nine, or ten years ago. For weeks and even months we investigated every lead that occurred to us. We interrogated every storekeeper who might have kept invoices of our purchases; checked with the gas and electric and telephone companies to see if they had kept records; interrogated physicians and dentists and opticians and medical laboratories that had served us; examined the monthly statements and other financial records of bank transactions; went to the County-City Building to look up voting registrations; interviewed innumerable friends and acquaintances who might remember my presence in the Seattle area during the three summers in question. Many kindly persons and even total strangers cooperated in our search. A heroic librarian, Dolly Cooper, searched thousands of books in the University of Washington Library to find in the back pocket of the books withdrawal cards, dated by a librarian, that I had signed, and was successful in discovering several crucial signatures and dates. Student volunteers scanned hundreds of newspapers from the musty files of the Seattle Public Library to find any possible references to my public lectures or other activities. Virginia and I were disappointed to discover that most memories are short and most records are not kept for longer than five or six years, but we were heartened by the fact that so many cooperated in our search. Gradually, with their generous assistance, we built up a formidable body of evidence against Hewitt, which we presented to the prosecuting attorney.

Canwell and John Boyd, deputy commissioner of the Immigration and Naturalization Service in the Department of Justice, approached Shorett and tried to dissuade him from filing the perjury charge. Hewitt had been a government witness in a number of deportation cases, and Boyd evidently wished to protect him as a future witness. Shorett was a man of stubborn integrity and resisted this pressure.

On August 10 the perjury charge was filed before William Hoar, Justice of the Peace. The prosecuting attorney had determined that there were just and adequate grounds for the indictment and submitted the proper information to the Justice Court. The complaint was reduced to writing, and I appeared before the court, swore to the complaint, and signed the papers. The usual legal procedure in the state of Washington was thus observed. In some states, it is the practice to bring an indictment through a grand jury, but in the state of Washington this method is rarely employed.

When the charge had been filed, Virginia and I decided that we needed a vacation. Having given up my summer-school job, I was short of money for living and vacation expenses. I applied to the National Bank of Commerce, where I had often borrowed in the past, but to my surprise I was refused a loan. A bank official, whom I knew as a friend, explained with some embarrassment that my tenure at the university appeared too insecure to justify the risk. Fortunately I was able to borrow enough money from my old friend, Brents Stirling, to make a short vacation possible. Since we owned no automobile, we loaded baggage and children onto a bus that took us to Port Angeles, on the Olympic Peninsula, and there we were picked up and driven to Olympic Hot Springs by arrangement with the resort manager. Thus we finally found ourselves deep in the mountains, where we swam in the pool, hiked over the ridges, and lounged in our cabin.

When we returned to Seattle after about two weeks, Virginia and I resumed the search for evidence. I had testified at the hearing that we had spent four or five weeks at Canyon Creek in the late summer of 1938, but we had not as yet proved that this was the case. We asked our friend Lenore Forbes, violinist in the Seattle Symphony, to drive us to the Canyon Creek area. First she drove us to the village of Arlington to see if any record had been kept of our overnight stay there when, in June, 1938, we had landed at the wrong destination. But the little hotel where we had slept had closed years ago, and no records were available. We then drove on to Canyon Creek and found, on entering the lodge, that it was under new management. The new owner, Thomas Grant, served us some soft drinks at the fountain, and we struck up a conversation with him. I broached the subject of our mission and explained that we wanted to check the lodge register.

"It isn't here," said Grant. "The investigators for the committee have carried it away."

Speechless, I jammed the straw down into my drink in shock and dismay. Virginia asked Grant if he had been given a receipt. "Yes," he said, "I have a written receipt."

Lenore then drove us to the residence of Mrs. Quincy Mueller, the former owner of the lodge, who had built an attractive home on the edge of Canyon Creek. She recalled our stay at the resort but was at first hesitant about the date. Her memory was refreshed when she recollected a conversation with Virginia about the old lodge, during which the two of them had walked down to the charred wreckage and poked around the ruins. Since the original lodge had burned in the spring of 1938 and the ruins were removed before the summer of 1939, Mrs. Mueller was positive that the date of our visit to Canyon Creek must have been the summer of 1938. Subsequently she wrote a letter to Prosecutor Shorett stating these facts.

After our interview with Mrs. Mueller, we drove to the home of Ida Kirby, the former caretaker, who lived at nearby Lake Stevens. From what she told us and from information that was later disclosed at the extradition hearing we were able to piece together the story. On

Saturday, July 24, the very next day after my testimony, a group of the committee's investigators, accompanied by uniformed members of the State Patrol, rushed to Canyon Creek Lodge and, with the help of Mrs. Kirby, searched the premises. They found a card from an index file with the notation: "Rader Mrs. Melvin M. (L) 8–16–40 Seattle, Wn. 6017 30th Avenue N.E. Prof at U of Washington Guest for 1 month." This card, with its date "8–16–40," was later introduced as an exhibit at the extradition hearing to show that we had been at the lodge in 1940, not in 1938 as I had testified.

On this very Saturday, before any contrary evidence was discovered, Mrs. Kirby signed an affidavit prepared by the committee's investigators fixing 1940 as the date of our visit to Canyon Creek.

Early on the following Monday, July 26, the investigators returned to the area. They obtained from Mrs. Mueller an affidavit stating that Mr. and Mrs. Melvin Rader had walked out to the lodge from Granite Falls "in the summer of 1939 or 1940," stayed a few days, and later returned "with considerable baggage and a small child." This affidavit, like that of Mrs. Kirby, contradicted my testimony that 1938 was the correct date. At the time that Mrs. Mueller signed this statement she knew nothing about conflicting evidence from the lodge register.

On this same Monday, July 26, the investigators persisted in their search of the lodge and, with the help of Ida Kirby, they at last found the register stuck away in the attic. As the men scanned the pages, Mrs. Kirby overheard one of them say, "There it is, Rader, '38." Leaving a receipt with Grant, the investigators carried away the index card and a packet of loose leaves from the register. Canwell and his staff never divulged this fact until many months had passed. They later made full use of the women's affidavits to "prove" their case even though the statements in the affidavits had been shown by the evidence from the lodge register to be inaccurate.

Mrs. Kirby, at our request, wrote to Shorett about the discovery of the register. The prosecutor planned to use both Mrs. Mueller and Mrs. Kirby as witnesses at Hewitt's trial.

Hewitt was still a fugitive from justice, and his arrest was not easy to arrange. As soon as the indictment was filed on August 10, Shorett sent to the New York police a copy of the warrant for the arrest together with information as to Hewitt's residence and place of employment. Hearing nothing in reply, Shorett finally wired the New York commissioner of police for an explanation. On October 19, he received a telegram from Martin J. Brown, chief inspector, stating: "George Hewitt case still under investigation. Will advise as soon as possible." On October 29, Shorett wired again for information and received a second reply from Inspector Brown: "George Hewitt has not been seen at given address. As soon as located will be apprehended." On November 4, Shorett wrote to Brown, asking for any information concerning Hewitt's whereabouts and enclosing a self-addressed stamped envelope for convenience in replying. There was no response to this letter. Finally on November 22, Shorett wrote to New York Mayor William O'Dwyer, setting forth all the above facts and concluding: "There is a tremendous public interest in this matter in Seattle. I dislike going over the head of the Police Department, but since you are a former District Attorney and have undoubtedly experienced delays of this kind yourself, may I ask you to use your good office in obtaining whatever information is available, and have the same transmitted to us? I will greatly appreciate your kindness in this regard." Mayor O'Dwyer did not reply.

During this period, when Hewitt "could not be located," his whereabouts were reported again and again in the New York press. He appeared as an expert witness in deportation hearings in New York City on August 30, September 15, and September 23. Late in September his employer Alfred Kohlberg complained to United States Attorney General Tom Clark that Communists were harassing Hewitt and that he needed police protection. On October 5, Deputy Immigration Commissioner John P. Boyd, who had tried to dissuade Shorett from filing the perjury charge, announced that the Immigration Service had asked the cooperation of the New York police in protecting Hewitt from harassment by Communists. On October 6, the Bronx police offered to assign a guard to protect Hewitt and his family, but this offer was declined by Mrs. Hewitt.

As I have already mentioned, the government's interest in protecting their witness might be explained in part by his involvement in the Hiss case. Acting as a one-man subcommittee of the House Un-American Activities Committee, Representative John McDowell (Republican, Pennsylvania) questioned Hewitt in the Federal Building in New York City on December 17. The *New York Sun* described Hewitt's disclosures to Representative McDowell as "highly important information" in the Whittaker Chambers–Alger Hiss case. Five days later Hewitt testified in the United States Court House in New York before the federal grand jury investigating Chambers' charges against Hiss.

All this information about Hewitt and more appeared

in the *New York Times*, the *Post*, the *Sun*, the *Herald Tribune* and the *World-Telegram*. Yet the New York police, in their communications with Prosecutor Shorett, reported that they could not find Hewitt! The Communists, as might be expected, seized upon this opportunity to impugn the integrity of the police. On December 22, the *Daily Worker* began to publish a series of front-page articles calling attention to Hewitt's public appearances, pointing out his home address and place of employment, and charging that the police were conniving with the F.B.I. to avoid arresting Hewitt on the perjury charge.

In the meantime there had been the 1948 electoral campaign with surprising consequences. Canwell ran for the State Senate on his record as chairman of the Un-American Activities Committee. His campaign leaflets were imprinted with the Communist hammer and sickle to symbolize the subversive forces over which he had triumphed. The leaflets also carried commendations by prominent organizations and citizens, including the head of the Board of Regents of the University of Washington, Joseph Drumheller, and the president of the university, Raymond B. Allen. Dr. Allen, as quoted, declared that the committee had neither abridged academic freedom nor "attempted to smear liberals with a red brush." We scarcely dared to hope that Canwell, with this kind of backing, could be defeated. Not only was he far better known than his opponent, but he was running for office in a conservative district. This was a year of political surprises, however, when Truman's victory over Dewey made the pollsters shake their heads incredulously. Even more startling to us in the state of Washington was the defeat of Canwell by a vote of 8,500 to 7,000. Two other members of his committee, Sydney Stevens and Thomas Bienz, were defeated in the elections, and only one, Grant Sisson, was re-elected. Still another member, R. L. Rutter, had resigned from the committee, privately expressing his unhappiness over its excessive expenditures and its use of George Hewitt as witness against me. Thus in a remarkably short time the committee had virtually ceased to exist. Finally it was killed completely during the next session of the legislature when the Republican House and the Democratic Senate were unable to reach agreement on a measure to reconstitute it.

Our reaction to another electoral victory was mixed. Lloyd Shorett, who had given us such strong support, was elected judge of the Superior Court. We felt that he deserved this victory, but we were afraid that his successor in the prosecutor's office might be far less committed to the justice of our case. Our anxiety was not allayed when the Republican county commissioners appointed Charles Carroll, a former All-American football player, to succeed Shorett. I never achieved rapport either with Carroll or with Frank Harrington, his chief deputy, who was assigned to the case. When E. M. Stenholm, the investigator for the prosecuting attorney, drove us to Canyon Creek to secure affidavits from Ida Kirby and Mrs. Mueller, he seemed to be carrying out a chore without much interest in the outcome.

On the morning of February 2 I received a telephone call from Brents Stirling. "Have you seen the morning paper?" he asked. "You had better rush out and buy a copy. All hell has broken loose." I hurried to the nearest newsstand and bought the paper.

The big story on the front page was a demand by County Commissioner Dean McLean that Carroll "resign in the public interest." McLean charged that Carroll had refused to dismiss the Hewitt case even though he had "been informed by bona fide representatives of the federal and state governments that the national security was involved." In a letter addressed to Carroll, McLean declared: "The first issue you raised in connection with the suggested dismissal was that it would cost you some thousands of left wing votes, and you asked how such votes would be made up should you become a candidate for Prosecutor or any other elective office. . . . At a subsequent meeting, however, you were shown bona fide evidence which, you said, convinced you that the case should be dismissed. You said you would do so. Instead of dismissing it, however, you stated at a still later meeting that you were committed to your predecessor, Lloyd Shorett, not to do so. You added that you were in conference with him to obtain a release from your commitment. . . . At a later meeting you stated that Shorett refused to release you from your commitment." According to McLean, Carroll subsequently agreed to dismiss the case because he was "convinced in the light of the evidence conviction would be impossible," but he finally reneged on his promise, still pleading commitment to his predecessor.

According to the prosecutor's version, Fred Niendorff of the *Post-Intelligencer* and Ed Stone, its managing editor, also demanded the dismissal of the case. Stone threatened: "We elected one prosecutor and we can defeat another. We will blast you right out of that office if you don't dismiss this case." Carroll replied (according to his own version), "Go ahead and start blasting." He also remarked that "no accredited government agency has publicly asked me to dismiss the case." (Note the word "publicly.")

The newspaper also contained a statement by Editor

Stone telling about a meeting in his office attended by Niendorff, Carroll, and McLean. At this meeting, according to Stone, Carroll expressed concern over the possible loss of "12,000 left wing votes." Stone asked, "What about the votes on the other side—the right side?" Carroll countered: "What do you mean?" Stone replied: "I mean that the *P-I* has taken on many battles for the good of the community, and usually wins." At this point, according to Stone, Carroll "took umbrage . . . and angrily rose to leave," but was persuaded by McLean to remain.

Having seen the statements by Carroll and Stone, McLean issued a further explanation. He said that he had been visited by representatives of the United States Department of Justice, and that Carroll himself had been approached by "a man speaking for the government." At the latter meeting, in Carroll's home, McLean heard the government spokesman plead "that Hewitt's testimony was vitally important in the prosecution of the 'pumpkin' spy cases and having to do with Communist espionage activities throughout the country." The spokesman complained that Hewitt's credibility as a witness would be impaired by the perjury charge, and that the indictment "would be used by the Communists to influence juries trying cases in which the national security was involved." McLean denied that either Stone or Niendorff had recommended dismissal of the case.

Finally the *Post-Intelligencer* quoted Judge Shorett: "My agreement with Carroll was that the case was not to be dismissed excepting if he became convinced that the charges were not well founded. I was under great political pressure to dismiss the case, and similar pressure has been put on him."

The final report of the Canwell Committee was submitted to the State Legislature on February 3, 1949. As

Virginia and I read the report, we could hardly believe our eyes. It declared that the precise date of my presence at the Briehl's Farm school was 1938, that my first visit to Canyon Creek was in August, 1940, that a federal agency had produced two witnesses who verified Hewitt's charges, and that it was not Hewitt but I who had lied before the committee. The report also cast wholly unjustified aspersions against my attorneys and recommended some highly repressive legislation. All this was said under the protection of "legislative immunity" against a libel suit.

I immediately issued a reply: "The statements made about me by the Canwell committee in its report to the legislature are in substance entirely false. . . . If the Canwell committee think the contrary, why are they not willing to have their witness, George Hewitt, stand trial in a fair and open court? I would welcome such a court test because I know that I am telling the truth and that George Hewitt is not."

About this time Tom C. Clark, the attorney general of the United States, was approached with a request to use his influence to secure dismissal of the charges against Hewitt. Strong pressure was also exerted upon Governor Thomas E. Dewey not to authorize Hewitt's extradition. But neither Clark nor Dewey was willing to bow to this pressure.

Years later in 1962 or 1963, Ed Guthman (then chief press agent for Attorney General Robert Kennedy) discussed these events with Clark, who was at that time justice of the United States Supreme Court. When Guthman recalled that Prosecutor Carroll had privately stated to federal officials in 1949 that he would dismiss the charges against Hewitt if the attorney general should so request, Clark remembered that he had been asked to intervene and had refused. "I felt that it was something the attorney general of the United States shouldn't do," he said, "and I didn't do it."

What was the explanation of this amazing sequence of events? Why had so much pressure been put upon two prosecutors of King County, the governor of New York, and the attorney general of the United States? Why had the New York commissioner of police and the mayor of New York been so unresponsive to appeals for Hewitt's arrest? Why had the police replied to Shorett that they could not find Hewitt when his whereabouts were being reported in half a dozen newspapers? Why had the Canwell Committee in its report to the State Legislature so grossly misrepresented the facts?

The explanation appears to be obvious. The Canwell Committee and its allies wanted to protect their witness, and the Department of Justice wanted to shield one of its professional informers. In addition Hewitt was being groomed as a witness against Alger Hiss. It must have seemed very important to prevent his arrest and clear his name so that he could testify in the forthcoming trial. The conviction of Hiss would be political dynamite.

I do not know what Hewitt would have testified against Hiss in an open court. His secret testimony before Representative McDowell of the House Committee on Un-American Activities and before the federal grand jury has never been disclosed. But we do know that there were ties between Hewitt and Hiss's other accusers. One of the first to bring charges against Hiss was Hewitt's employer, Alfred Kohlberg, wealthy importer from China and publisher of *Plain Talk* magazine. In late 1947 and March, 1948, Kohlberg accused Hiss of Communist affiliation in letters to John Foster Dulles, adviser to the State Department and board chairman of the Carnegie Endowment for International Peace. Since Hiss was at that time president of the endowment, these attacks were clearly intended to undermine his position. The editor of Kohlberg's magazine, Isaac Don Levine, was one of Whittaker Chambers' friends and associates. As early as August, 1939, Levine introduced Chambers to Roosevelt's White House Secretary Marvin H. McIntyre, to whom Chambers divulged his initial charges against Hiss. Then on September 2, 1939, Levine accompanied Chambers to Adolf Berle, assistant secretary of state, where the charges were repeated. Levine himself testified on December 8, 1948, before the House Committee on Un-American Activities in support of Chambers. Another member of the *Plain Talk* circle and contributor to the magazine was Howard Rushmore. It was he, as the reader will recall, who made the first public disclosure of the impending charges against Hiss when he testified before the Canwell Committee.

All of these men—Kohlberg, Hewitt, Levine, Chambers, and Rushmore—were Cold Warriors of the Far Right, and all except Kohlberg were former members of the Communist Party. Rushmore and Levine, in addition, were frequent contributors to the Hearst press, which through Fred Niendorff had important links with Canwell and Houston. In view of these ties, it appeared to have been no accident that Rushmore and Hewitt were star witnesses before the Canwell Committee.

I have often wondered whether Hewitt's secret testimony against Hiss was as false and perjured as his testimony against me, and whether the campaign that ruined Alger Hiss was "hatched" in Alfred Kohlberg's office.

9

Purge

WHILE the various events narrated in the preceding chapter were going on, I was trying to concentrate on research and writing. During the autumn of 1948 I was on leave from university teaching under my grant from the Rockefeller Foundation. The subject of my research—the nature of historical crisis—stirred me deeply. I read many articles and books—such as those of Marx, Toynbee, Sorokin, and Mannheim—that sought to probe the malaise of civilizations, and what I learned affected my teaching and writing for years to come.

My own predicament and that of others lent a strange poignancy to this research. Not only had I and my family suffered from the tensions and hostilities of a period of crisis, but every newspaper that I picked up, every radio broadcast that I heard, told of similar or related events. "Loyalty" investigations and "anti-Communist" campaigns had become a national obsession. The Hiss case was only the most prominent of thousands of "cases." The testimony of innumerable informers, such as Elizabeth Bentley, Freda Utley, and Louis Budenz, provided sensational headlines in every newspaper. As early as July 21, 1948, J. Edgar Hoover announced that more than two million federal employees had been investigated under the "loyalty program." Many individuals in both public and private employment lost their jobs, and the political campaigns of 1948 rang loudly with denunciations of "subversive forces." Many newspapers and periodicals joined in the hue and cry, and a false standard of Americanism—the uncritical and unquestioning acceptance of things as they are—was dinned into people's minds.

I believed in a very different method of preserving free institutions. The best defense against antidemocratic forces, it seemed to me, was a dynamic democratic program that would bring hope and exhilaration and happiness "in widest commonalty spread." The quaint language of the *Tao Te Ching*, ancient scripture of Chinese Taoism, caught the spirit of this positive approach: "Make the people's food sweet, their clothes beautiful, their houses comfortable, their daily life a source of pleasure. Then the people will look at the country over the border, will hear the cocks crowing and the dogs barking there, but right down to old age and the day of their death, they will not trouble to go there and see what it is like." This, said Lao Tze, is the way to inculcate loyalty.

How different was the wave of intolerance that was sweeping through the land, and how different was the actual course of events in Seattle! Seven of the witnesses before the Canwell Committee were tried for contempt, and six of them were convicted. Five were sentenced to 30 days in jail and fined $250. Mrs. Burton James, the one exception among the convicted witnesses, was given a suspended sentence of 30 days and fined $125. Other accused individuals lost their jobs or were subjected to further loyalty investigations. The Seattle Repertory Theater, which had been subjected to heavy attack during the hearing, was boycotted and forced out of business.

On September 8, the university administration filed charges against six faculty members who had been accused of Communist affiliation by witnesses before the Canwell Committee. I believe I would have been charged along with the others if there had been no perjury indictment against Hewitt. The faculty tenure committee conducted protracted hearings on the charges, compiling thirty-two volumes of testimony. President Allen negotiated unsuccessfully with Whittaker Chambers and Louis Budenz to appear as prosecution witnesses, but two other prominent ex-Communists, Joseph Kornfedder and Benjamin Gitlow, testified about the inner workings of the American Communist Party. In effect, the Party was being tried, and not the individual teachers as such.

Three of the men under fire—Melville Jacobs in the Anthropology Department, Garland Ethel and Harold Eby in the English Department—admitted past membership in the Communist Party but denied present membership. During their appearance before the Canwell Committee, they had been forthright in testifying about themselves but had refused to inform upon others. Their response to the threat of contempt proceedings was typified by Eby's words: "I find that I couldn't face myself and live any more, if I were to name people that are my friends and associates, who as far as I know are honorable and loyal." All three left the Communist Party voluntarily because they could not believe in its principles. I knew and respected these men, and I regarded their prosecution by the university administration as a gross violation of academic freedom.

A fourth man—Ralph Gundlach of the Psychology Department—refused on grounds of conscience and civil liberties to testify about his political affiliations before the Canwell Committee, but when he testified before the tenure committee he denied having ever been a Communist. I believed then, and I still believe, in the honesty of his declaration: "I learned that human personality and individuality and kindly human relationships are the important values; that human rights are a means of safeguarding the conditions for general human development; and that our institutions in society are not ends in themselves, but means, for the service of the needs of mankind. So, I am anti-fascist, anti-authoritarian; a democrat; a humanitarian; in the broad, deep sense, a Christian." I had often heard Ralph repeat Kant's "categorical imperative" that one should treat human beings as ends in themselves, never merely as means. This seemed to me the essence of antitotalitarian doctrine.

A fifth man, Joseph Butterworth, testified to the tenure committee that he was presently a Communist. There was no evidence submitted that his teaching of Chaucer and Old English had been affected by his politics, or that he was academically incompetent, or that he had ever performed a subversive or an illegal act. I thought of him as a tragic figure—a crippled and lonely man, whose wife had committed suicide and whose only child had been committed to an institution. There were more charitable ways to deal with his case.

Herbert Phillips, the sixth man, was known to almost everybody by his nickname "Scoop." I knew him intimately as my colleague in the Philosophy Department. Rather short, dark, and ruddy-faced, characterized by energetic gestures and a friendly manner, he was a most engaging member of the faculty. He had an inexhaustible fund of witty stories, a shrewd capacity to penetrate into another person's mind, and superb skill in philosophical argument. Although a member of the Communist Party, he was too much the philosopher to renounce his intellectual independence. It was typical of him that his favorite textbook for the introductory course was W. E. Hocking's *Types of Philosophy*, written from an un-Marxian and idealistic point of view, and that the contemporary philosopher he admired most was Alfred North Whitehead, whose interpretation of reality would be looked at askance by most Communists.

By temperament he was a candid person, who announced to his classes that he was a Marxist. Almost everybody on the campus knew that he was a Communist, although they were not told in so many words that he carried a Party card. William Savery, the chairman of our department, used to say to him: "Scoop, I don't know whether you are a member of the Communist Party or not, but if you are, I don't want to know it. The university administration might fire you if you were known to be a Communist, and I wouldn't lie to them if they should inquire. So if you are a Communist, keep your mouth shut!"

In saying this, Savery was not motivated by sympathy for the Communist Party—in fact, he detested it. But he believed that freedom of thought and association is the basis of liberal democracy, and that a man's politics, so long as he is law-abiding, are his own business. Even after Savery died late in 1946, this was the attitude of his colleagues in the Philosophy Department. All of us testified before the tenure committee that Phillips was a gifted teacher and an independent philosopher.

I enjoyed him as a friend and regarded him as a valuable member of our staff. He and I had many conversations about philosophy and politics; he impressed me with his sincerity and intellectual zest; and we worked together in the Teachers' Union. Although we agreed about many things we sharply disagreed about others. I respected his right to differ from the orthodox in his convictions and associations, and I was strongly opposed to his dismissal. His candid statement of his beliefs and affiliations before the tenure committee made me respect him the more.

These were the six heretics charged by the administration. The university admitted that they were not being tried in their professional capacity. At the outset of the hearing the administration's statement declared: "We will indulge in the conclusive presumption that every person here charged is sufficiently learned in his field and sufficiently skillful in his teaching, and that he is not using the classroom as a forum for the indoctrination of his students into communism, or anything similar thereto." It was clear to everyone that the men were charged because of pressure stemming from the Canwell Committee, and that the complaint was that they were or had been members of the Communist Party. As a majority of the tenure committee pointed out, there was nothing in the university's tenure code that authorized this kind of prosecution.

The code, which represented a "gentleman's agreement" between the faculty and the Board of Regents, prescribed that the trial should take place before the Faculty Committee on Tenure and Academic Freedom. It also provided for the manner of trial: "The accused shall be entitled to representation during his trial by any person of his choice. . . . The accused shall be confronted with the witnesses against him, shall be privileged to be present at all sessions of the Committee when testimony is being heard, shall have the right to call and examine witnesses and to produce relevant documents in his behalf, and to cross-examine witnesses produced against him." These procedural safeguards, which were very different from the procedures of the Canwell Committee, were faithfully observed.

In accordance with the specified right to make its additional procedural rules, the tenure committee decided that the prolonged hearings should be secret. This secrecy was opposed by Phillips and Butterworth, with Phillips going so far as to bring unsuccessful court action in an attempt to compel an open hearing. The sessions began on October 27 and continued with a few interruptions until December 15.

About half the time was taken up with an examination not of the six accused men but of the Communist Party. Counsel for the administration presented evidence designed to establish the general allegations made in the charges, namely, that the Communist Party is under the control of the Soviet Union, that it is undemocratic and dictatorial in its organizational structure, that its philosophy advocates the violent overthrow of established governments, that its members employ secret and fraudulent means, and that its program of immediate demands is designed to fool non-Communists into furthering the Communist cause.

The most important witnesses introduced to establish these allegations were Joseph Zack Kornfeder and Benjamin Gitlow. Kornfedder had been a charter member of the Communist Party until his expulsion in 1934; he had attended the Lenin Institute in Moscow as a member of the Central Committee of the American Communist Party, and he had worked for the Communist International in South America. Gitlow was a leading member of the Communist Party until his expulsion in 1929. His testimony was designed to show that the American Communist Party has been under the domination of Russia.

In rebuttal, attorneys for the accused professors maintained that Gitlow and Kornfedder had been expelled from the Communist Party so long ago that their testimony was no longer pertinent; that the evidence was irrelevant to any of the "causes for dismissal" set forth in the tenure code; and that as individuals the accused professors had not in fact been guilty of the alleged faults of the Communist Party.

The most distinguished witnesses in defense of the accused were Paul Sweezy and Edward Strong. Sweezy, formerly of the Department of Economics at Harvard University, was the author of articles and books on socialist and communist theory. He testified that Marxism and Leninism do not contain the doctrines ascribed to them by the university and presented alternative interpretations. Edward Strong, philosopher from the University of California at Berkeley and later provost during the tumultous "free speech" demonstrations of 1965, denied that the Marxist and Leninist theories have the sinister monolithic meaning ascribed to them by Gitlow and Kornfedder.

The remainder of the trial was devoted to the prosecution and defense of the individual respondents. Witnesses and testimonials were introduced to prove the honesty, moral integrity, and academic dutifulness and competency of the accused. For example, eleven witnesses testified in Phillips' behalf—five former students and six colleagues on the faculty. All of us members of the Philosophy Department testified to the high caliber of his teaching and scholarship, the objectivity of his presentation of controversial subjects, and his candor regarding his Marxist convictions. We testified that he had been so frank in expressing his opinions that none of us had been the least surprised to learn that he was a member of the Communist Party, although, following the departmental tradition, we had never questioned him as to his party affiliation. Similar evidence of moral integrity and professional competency was submitted in behalf of the other respondents. In addition the accused mounted the stand and testified at length in their own behalf.

The chief counsel for the university claimed that the heart of the tenure code was its definition of "tenure" as "the right of a person to hold his position during good behavior," and that membership in the Communist Party entails "bad behavior." In addition there were some specific charges against individuals among the accused, namely, that they had been less than frank or honest in their interviews with President Allen, or that they had not been sufficiently cooperative with the Canwell Committee. Four persons, all of whom had appeared as friendly witnesses at the Canwell Committee hearing, testified that Ralph Gundlach, despite his denial, was a member of the Communist Party. Dean Edwin Guthrie of the Graduate School also testified that Gundlach had been evasive in his interview with President Allen prior to the Canwell hearing. But the main charge throughout the trial was that membership in the Communist Party constitutes bad behavior and is itself ground for dismissal.

I did not hear the procedures except when I was personally present as a witness, but I did hear the final summation of the attorneys on both sides. It was decided that a representative of each of the departments involved should be present, and since Everett Nelson, chairman of the Philosophy Department, was away at the time, I was appointed by the university administration as acting chairman and served in his stead. Newspaper reporters were also invited, and I was more than a little angry when, on the following morning, Fred Niendorff's account in the *Post-Intelligencer* mentioned that I had been there, leaving the implication that I was among the suspects who might be dismissed.

On January 22 the Board of Regents acted, contrary for the most part to the recommendations of a majority of the tenure committee. The two self-admitted Communists, Phillips and Butterworth, and the one person who denied ever having been a member of the Party, Gundlach, were discharged summarily without severance pay. The three who had left the Party voluntarily, Eby, Ethel, and Jacobs, were required to sign disclaimer affidavits and were put on probation for two years. I was among 103 members of the faculty who protested these actions as a violation of academic freedom, and the national office of the American Association of University Professors, after very protracted debate and delay, reached the same conclusion.

When the decisions of the regents were announced, there was a great hubbub of excitement on our campus and in academic communities all over America. In publications such as the *American Scholar* and the *New York Times*, some of the foremost intellectual leaders in America discussed the issues. No one analyzed the question

[115]

more cogently than Arthur E. Murphy of Cornell University. As a visiting professor in our department and a distinguished philosopher, he was invited to give the annual Phi Beta Kappa address. Although no copy of this address is available, the essence of his remarks was repeated in a symposium later held at the Yale Law School: "If the test we use in judging academic competence is applied to each individual on his own merits, or lack of them, if it is a test that is genuinely relevant to the adequate performance of his function as a truth seeker, and if it is applied by those both qualified and concerned to judge on just this point, then we have stood our ground and kept the faith that was entrusted to us. If it is applied to men in groups, or sects, or parties, on the basis of their political affiliations and in response to external pressures and anxieties in which the demand for doctrinal conformity has a major part, then it is a surrender by the University of its own proper standards and responsibility, a surrender that is also a betrayal." Murphy believed, and his colleagues in the Philosophy Department agreed, that there had been just this sort of betrayal at the University of Washington.

I have always been intensely proud of being a member of our university faculty. There is no earthly institution more splendid than a university, and no country is lost so long as its universities are free. There is nothing finer in the whole tradition of civil liberties than the ideal expressed by Thomas Jefferson in founding the University of Virginia: "This institution will be based upon the illimitable freedom of the human mind. For here we are not afraid to follow truth wherever it may lead, nor to tolerate error so long as reason is left free to combat it." This is the way I conceive a university, and the colleagues I respect most have clung tenaciously to this conception. In a time when every future looked grim and every value was threatened, the University of Washington was untrue to Jefferson's ideal. We liberals on the faculty have struggled to restore our institution to the tradition of academic freedom, and in the course of years we have in great measure succeeded. We have rid ourselves of loyalty probes and oaths and bans against radical speakers, and we are about as free as any state university in America.

10

A

Time of

Uncertainty

During the tenure hearing and its aftermath, Herbert Schneider of Columbia University and I were trying to arrange an exchange for the forthcoming academic year 1949–50. In the spring of 1946 he had been a visiting professor in the Philosophy Department at the University of Washington. Although quiet and unassuming, he had impressed everyone with his charm and erudition. He loved the Puget Sound country and was anxious to return. Virginia and I, who had lived almost all of our lives in the West, looked forward just as eagerly to the adventure of a year in New York. Since the Schneider and Rader families were comparable in size, we planned to exchange houses as well as teaching positions. For a while both universities appeared cooperative, and there seemed to be no difficulty in making the arrangements.

In a letter written on January 23, 1949, Professor Schneider discussed our mutual plans and the recent firings. "The University news is indeed shocking," he said, "and I can well imagine how disturbed you must all be. . . . I imagine that under these circumstances you will be glad to be gone next year. I hate being in such a mess myself, but coming as outsider to the conflict, I can live in it better than you can. I fear it would be a hypocritical gesture for me to refuse to come, since Columbia has fired men for no better reasons and not too long ago! However, if I teach a course in social and political philosophy, I shall be obliged to speak my mind." He then commented on such practical details as the time of moving.

There was one element of uncertainty in the negotiations—the "Hewitt-Rader case" had been called to the attention of the Columbia authorities, and they were quite perturbed. On February 12, Professor Schneider wrote: "President Allen was in town recently and apparently talked to some of our deans or provost in such a way as to give them the impression that in all probability the court proceedings in which you are involved may drag on into the coming academic year and that you would probably not be free to come. Under such circumstances they want to play safe and call off the exchange for next year now, before the announcements go to press finally. *So*—we really need more information here. First of all, I'd like to know what *you* know and how you feel about the whole business. Secondly, if Allen gave the Columbia authorities a wrong impression somebody in authority at the University of Washington ought to set them straight at once. They are scared, now!" Schneider ended his letter with the remark, "I'm sorry things are so up in the air here and so down in the dumps there. Are there good reasons for postponing the exchange?"

In response I asked President Allen to write to Columbia, and I fired back an optimistic telegram, but Schneider replied on February 20 with another gloomy letter. "The authorities here," he wrote, "are timid about 'publicity' and legal complications. . . . I don't see that they are making any effort to look into the merits of the Washington situation; on the contrary, they don't want to be informed! They claim the political issue has nothing to do with the case." Despite this claim, the Columbia officials refused to approve the exchange until the "legal procedures" were over. Unfortunately the "legal procedures" could be dragged out indefinitely, since there was no assurance that Hewitt would soon be extradited and brought to trial.

President Allen waited until February 21 to write to Provost Albert C. Jacobs of Columbia, and his letter was not very reassuring. The most important paragraph was the following: "Professor Rader, as you know, has a distinguished record at this University and he is currently Acting Executive Officer of the Department of Philosophy in the absence this term of Professor Nelson. Quite understandably he is seriously disturbed over Hewitt's charges and is eager to have this matter cleared up as soon as possible. I sincerely hope that this transpires for him and the University." The president's letter did nothing to change the minds of the Columbia authorities.

While these messages were being exchanged, the hope that Hewitt would be brought to trial began to revive. On February 9 the chief investigator for the Canwell Committee, John Whipple, reported in the *Seattle Post-Intelligencer* that he had received a long-distance telephone call from Hewitt's wife announcing that her husband would return to Seattle voluntarily as soon as legal counsel could be arranged for him. Whipple said that the Un-American

Activities Committee itself was anxious that the case should go to trial. Somewhat ominously he predicted that the Hewitt trial would "open up some things that need airing out at the University of Washington." The next day, on February 10, Hewitt surrendered to the New York City police; but he was promptly released pending a hearing, and he announced that he would fight extradition.

In Seattle, Prosecutor Carroll and his chief deputy Frank Harrington began preparing extradition papers after being notified by telegram of Hewitt's surrender. Washington Governor Arthur Langlie then forwarded the papers to New York Governor Thomas E. Dewey, who executed the rendition warrant on February 22. Before action on the warrant was taken, Alfred Kohlberg, Hewitt's employer, approached the American Civil Liberties Union to enlist support for Hewitt's defense. When Virginia and I heard that the firm of Theodore Diamond and Carl Rachlin, who often acted as attorneys for the A.C.L.U., had agreed to act as Hewitt's counsel, we were astounded by the boldness and success of Kohlberg's maneuver. It was shocking to us that the liberals would lend their support to a perjurer for an antilibertarian committee.

The Seattle branch of the American Civil Liberties Union, however, rallied to our aid. Its president, Professor John W. Richards of the University of Washington Law School, wrote a letter of protest to Herbert M. Levy, staff counsel at the A.C.L.U. national office. Another representative of the Seattle chapter, Charles Larrowe, also communicated with Levy and, at the latter's suggestion, wrote to Diamond. Larrowe stated in his letter that Prosecutor Shorett, who had brought the charge of perjury against Hewitt, was "strongly anti-Communist" and, to be sure that I was no Communist, had insisted on "a very thorough investigation" including a check by the F.B.I. "I am sure you will be interested to know," Larrowe concluded, "that Messrs. Lloyd Shorett, Edward Henry, and Paul Coughlin are all members of our local chapter of the A.C.L.U." The enclosures that accompanied the letter explained in detail the nature and grounds of the perjury charge against Hewitt.

Finally Henry telephoned Carl Rachlin and talked with him at length. Since he was conversing with the "opposite side," Henry spoke with caution. He was hopeful that Hewitt would be brought to trial, and he thought it was important not to give away the case to the opposition. Hewitt forewarned would be Hewitt forearmed: to counter our evidence he might plead a case of mistaken identity or invent some other lies. Rachlin, not understanding our case, refused to budge. As he later explained, the evidence in support of Hewitt's testimony appeared strong, and—without knowledge of counterevidence—he and Mr. Diamond concluded that, if there were any civil liberties issues involved, they appeared to be in Hewitt's favor. Diamond and Rachlin acted as private attorneys, and the American Civil Liberties Union declined to intervene on either side. At the time Virginia and I did not understand that the union, as such, was taking no part in the case, and we were dumbfounded at what we thought was transpiring.

Puzzled by events in New York, I enlisted the aid of Herbert's wife, Grenafore Schneider, in the effort to investigate. Grenafore, who had worked as assistant supervisor of recreation for the New York Park Department, was a practical and determined lady. She set out at once to discover what was afoot. On March 25 she wrote to me reporting an interview with Hewitt's attorney: "Mr. Rachlin says his firm has handled civil liberties cases before and hopes this will be one—he says that he has 'not received a penny so far' and Mr. Hewitt is fighting because his wife and three children will starve or become relief cases if his $35 a week multigraph operator job is interrupted by a journey west. Mr. Rachlin says his client has affidavits of other persons to the effect that Mr. Rader was not in his mountain camp in 1938 as he alleges but was actually seen in New York at the Kingston School where Mr. Hewitt (Timothy Holmes) was teaching, and that Mr. Rader is making a bad mistake. He says that only political pressure by red groups in Seattle on the district attorney keeps him from withdrawing the warrant, because there is really no case against Mr. Hewitt."

An extradition hearing had been set for March 10 but was postponed. At the rescheduled hearing on March 24, Rachlin requested and secured a continuance until the thirty-first of March. Mrs. Schneider on March 25 reported: "Neither the chief clerk nor the D.A.'s office had any record of the hearing scheduled for yesterday. . . . There is much delay, many adjournments and obvious reluctance to stand trial in Seattle. The case seems to be kept unpublicized and unlisted as much as possible. It is hard to find out where hearings are to be heard—'Why do you want to know? What is your interest in the case?' are frequently asked. Justice seems to be blind still!" On March 31 Mrs. Schneider showed up for the rescheduled extradition hearing, and there was still another postponement.

"I wish I could write better news," Herbert Schneider said in a letter of April 3, "but, no doubt, so do you!

Grenafore found out that the next hearing for Hewitt's extradition would be May 12th. His lawyer may appeal even then, to gain another six months. In any case, I see no end to this thing! Do you have a summer term of courts? If not, the case is sure to drag into next year. Have you any inclination to drop the whole affair? Or could you, if you wanted to? . . . It is a nuisance to all concerned to be unable to plan definitely. What is your advice?"

On April 6 I replied: "You ask if I have any inclination to drop the case. My answer is, No. In the first place, it is not my private case: the State of Washington has charged Hewitt with perjury, and not I as an individual. But even if I could induce the prosecuting attorney to drop the case —which perhaps I could do—I would certainly not do so. I am entirely innocent of the accusations that Hewitt has made. He has, in my opinion, deliberately lied, and I would certainly not be a party to clearing his name, especially when such action might be interpreted as a confession of guilt on my part."

But I realized that the time was already late to decide on the exchange of teaching positions, and that the Columbia authorities were understandably impatient. "I suppose it would be best to abandon our plans for next year," I wrote in the same letter. "I am reluctant to give up the idea of going to New York some time or other. But of course I want to do that which will be entirely satisfactory to you and Grenafore and the children and to the Columbia Department." This decision was a bitter pill. In the previous summer I had resigned my appointment at the University of California so as to press the charges against Hewitt, and now I had to surrender an opportunity that was even more attractive.

The news reports in the Seattle papers were contradictory and confusing. After Hewitt gave himself up to the New York police on February 10, Prosecutor Carroll immediately announced to the *Post-Intelligencer* that his office would "treat this case just like any other in which a person is charged with crime," that the state would if necessary foot the bill to bring Hewitt back to Seattle, and that Captain Wendell B. Norris of the sheriff's staff would be sent east to return Hewitt when he had been extradited. But on March 11 Carroll stated in the *P-I*, "I haven't any of the money of the King County taxpayers to send witnesses and an extradition agent to sit around New York and wouldn't spend it that way if I had it." Then on May 4 the startling news appeared in the *Seattle Times* that Hewitt denied that he was Hewitt. "New York authorities tell me that the man under arrest denies everything," said Carroll. "He denies he is Hewitt and denies he appeared before the [Canwell] Committee." The prosecutor repeated his statement that he had no money to spend on extradition. Explaining that it would be necessary to send witnesses from Seattle to identify Hewitt, he concluded, "We don't have that kind of money, so can't send the witnesses, but it looks doubtful if we can extradite Hewitt without doing so."

As a result of Carroll's decision, District Attorney Samuel J. Foley of Bronx County, New York, was informed that the state of Washington did not intend to send a representative or submit evidence to the New York extradition hearing. This was a clear signal that there would be no contest against a one-sided and inaccurate presentation of the facts, and no obstruction to a refusal to extradite. When Hewitt's attorney, Carl Rachlin, received this information it confirmed his belief in Hewitt's innocence.

Later, in a letter of explanation to Paul Coughlin dated October 24, 1949, Rachlin declared: "Our opinion of the flimsy nature of the Washington charges was substantiated when we were informed by the District Attorney of Bronx County that the State of Washington did not intend to send a representative to the New York proceeding, and that no evidence was to be submitted either to refute Hewitt's contention that extradition was predicated on political motives, or to overcome his proof of the truth of his original statements."

During this period Ralph Gundlach was in New York City trying to present District Attorney Samuel J. Foley with decisive evidence. As the reader will recall, Hewitt had testified before the Canwell Committee that both Gundlach and I had been present at the Briehl's Farm school for a "six weeks intensive study of Marxism-Leninism," and that Hewitt finally identified the period as in the summer of 1938. Gundlach, acting through New York attorney Murray Gordon, sought to present evidence to Foley, based upon the records of the University of Washington, that would have refuted Hewitt's story and exposed him as a perjurer. The evidence revealed that the University of Washington summer school in 1938 lasted practically all summer and was divided into two independent sessions, that I had taught the first part of the summer, and Gundlach the second. Hence Hewitt's sworn testimony that we both were present at Briehl's Farm for the six-week period was obviously false. Dr. Gundlach was ready and eager to present this and other supporting evidence, but District Attorney Foley refused to consider it. When Gundlach, through counsel, asked Foley if he might testify, the district attorney neither questioned nor summoned him. After the date of the extradition hearing had been shifted several times, Foley failed to notify either Gundlach or his attorney of the final correct date. Although I had been informed that Ralph was in New York, I was not aware of his attempt to approach the district attorney. Also I failed to realize at this time how clinching was his evidence. Even if I had realized, I might have had no more success in approaching Foley than Gundlach and his counsel had.

Rebuffing the effort of Gundlach to supply crucial information, Foley remained ignorant of the true facts concerning my teaching activities in the summer of 1938. Later, in the course of the extradition hearing, he declared that the official records of the University proved that I had terminated my teaching services on June 20, 1938, and did not resume teaching until September, 1938. Evidently Foley had never been supplied with the record of my summer school employment, and mistakenly concluded that the record he had received was complete. He may never have suspected that the Canwell Committee had supplied him with incomplete and misleading data.

As the extradition hearing date of May 12 approached, I had a number of conferences with my attorneys as to what I should do. They pointed out to me that the facts were discouraging. Not only did the New York situation look unpromising, but Charles Carroll apparently had no intention of vigorously pursuing the case. As my attorneys reminded me, he had declared that his office had no money to spend on Hewitt's extradition, and that he would not spend the taxpayers' money in that way even if he had it to spare. It seemed folly to depend upon him for the return of Hewitt to Seattle or for an earnest prosecution of the case. An unwilling or inept prosecution might be worse than none.

I had no money of my own for a trip to New York, and it was questionable whether I could accomplish anything if I went. I might spend a good deal of money traveling back to New York only to find that there would be another protracted delay. Every indication pointed to the attempt to postpone and evade.

There was still the hope that the court would abide by the Constitution of the United States and the laws of the state of New York. The Constitution provides: "A person charged in any state with treason, felony, or other crime, who shall flee from justice, and be found in another state, shall on demand of the executive authority of the state from which he fled, be delivered up to be removed to the state having jurisdiction of the crime." In interpreting what is admissible in an extradition hearing, the United States Supreme Court ruled: "When the extradition papers required by the statute are in the proper form the only evidence sanctioned by this court as admissible on such a hearing is such as tends to prove that the accused was not in the demanding state at the time the crime is alleged to have been committed. . . . Defenses cannot be entertained on such a hearing, but must be referred for investigation to the trial of the case in the courts of the demanding state" (*Biddinger* v. *Commissioner of Police*, 245 U.S. 129, year 1917). The New York Court of Appeals, highest court in the state, supported this ruling. It declared that the only question open in such proceedings is "whether 'the extradition papers required by statute are in the proper form.' . . . Nothing more is required" (*People ex. rel. Gellis* v. *Sheriff of Westchester County*, 351 N.Y. 33, 166 N.E. 795, year 1929). Although I did not know the wording of these decisions, I was told that evidence bearing on the guilt or innocence of Hewitt would be legally inadmissible at the extradition hearing.

If the court were to abide by the law and honor the extradition warrant, Virginia and I would move heaven and earth to convict Hewitt. We were prepared to beg or borrow whatever money was necessary and to rally whatever forces we could muster to see that justice was done. But my attorneys, Coughlin and Henry, were not optimistic about the possibility of a victorious trial. They pointed out that it is notoriously easy to escape a perjury conviction. All that is required is somehow to invent a plausible story of mistaken identity or other "honest" error. I believed so vehemently in the strength of our case that I found it difficult to accept this opinion, but I was impressed by the knowledge and intelligence of the attorneys and I was discouraged by Carroll's attitude.

After weighing the advice of my lawyers, Virginia and I decided on an alternative plan of action. We had conclusive evidence that Hewitt had not told the truth, and if there was to be no trial we could submit this evidence to the university and, through the news media, ultimately to the public. Hewitt and the Canwell Committee would thus be exposed, and I would be vindicated.

We found it difficult to reconcile ourselves to this plan. For so many weeks and months we had hoped and schemed and labored to bring Hewitt to justice and thus to strike a mighty blow against the Canwell Committee and its ilk. Now we were compelled to acknowledge that the force of argument supported a different course of action. With the most profound reluctance in the world, we decided to do nothing until after the forthcoming extradition hearing. When the hearing described in the next chapter took place, I was three thousand miles from the scene, but I was later able to reconstruct what had happened from the official transcript and an eye-witness account sent to me by Grenafore Schneider.

11

The

Extradition

Hearing

WANTED for perjury in the second degree, George Hewitt appeared at the Bronx County Court House in the custody of his attorney, Carl Rachlin. The district attorney of the county, Mr. Samuel J. Foley, himself represented the state of New York. He was aided by the assistant district attorney, John B. Lee. The principals chatted amiably together while the audience gathered. Finally the honorable Aaron J. Levy, a white-haired gentleman in judicial robes, rapped for order, and the court convened.

Mr. Rachlin, young, slender, reddish-haired, moved that the certified minutes of the 1948 Hearing of the Washington State Un-American Activities Committee and its Report to the 31st Washington Legislature be added to the record. Judge Levy saw no objection, and the motion was granted.

Addressing the court, Mr. Foley narrated the history of the events that had culminated in Hewitt's arrest and his application for a writ of habeas corpus. He explained the appearance of Hewitt at the un-American activities hearing in the state of Washington and the nature of his testimony that Melvin Rader had been one of his students at the Briehl's Farm school, to which no one could be admitted unless he was a member of the Communist Party.

Prior to this testimony in the Seattle hearing, Mr. Rader had been confronted by Hewitt in the chambers of the committee and had been questioned by its chairman, but he made no denial of the charges thus divulged in advance. "There is in the record the evidence that he displayed no indignation; he did not seek to come back and further confront; he waived the right to cross-examination that was offered to him personally. . . . For these several days, the two days during which the testimony was taken of Hewitt, Rader testifying on the second day, and for two or three days subsequently thereto, he had every opportunity to bring the authorities, while this man was in that jurisdiction, whatever of complaint he had." This Rader failed to do. When the committee asked if he would cooperate with their investigators in an effort to establish the truth, he refused this offer—although he said he would cooperate with others who might be approved by his own counsel. "The Committee undertook its independent investigation, and the result of that investigation indicates that the professor lied."

Continuing, Mr. Foley said that Mr. Rader, in his own testimony at the hearing, declared that he had taught in the 1938 summer session at the University of Washington, but the evidence was to the contrary. "We have here photostatic copies of records of the payroll of the University of Washington for the whole year of 1938, and they

[131]

are attested by the Assistant Comptroller of the University, and have been made a part of the record of this Joint Legislative Committee of the State of Washington. They show that the faculty was paid on a ten-month basis, September first to June 30th, but they were paid additionally for the summer session, and the summer school began on the dates indicated—and Professor Rader terminated his paid services on the 20th of June, 1938, and did not resume until the first of September, 1938."

Mr. Rader had further testified that for part of that summer he was at Canyon Creek Lodge with his wife and child, but there were photostatic copies of affidavits here from people who operated this Canyon Creek Lodge, or who worked in it. "And it is their testimony that Professor Rader never appeared at that Lodge before the summer of 1940."

"So that, by the affidavits submitted and the documentary evidence, I agree with the conclusion of the Committee that the Professor did not tell the truth upon the stand. . . . Now, your Honor, the charge here is perjury, and the charge of perjury is made by a man whose own integrity under oath is assailed by a unanimous report of a Joint Committee of the Legislature, bipartisan in its politics, but unanimous in its lack of faith in his veracity."

Mr. Foley then read from the Report of the Committee to the Thirty First Session of the Washington Legislature: "In the case of Melvin Rader, Associate Professor of Philosophy at the University of Washington, the Committee's investigating staff and an agency of the Federal Government have produced evidence showing conclusively that Professor Rader did not tell the truth when he testified before the Committee. . . . Mr. Rader testified that during the period in question he taught at the University of Washington summer school and that he spent a vacation at Canyon Creek Lodge near Granite Falls. Your Committee's investigators have established that Mr. Rader's first appearance at Canyon Creek Lodge was in August of 1940, and that there was a six-weeks' period when he did not teach summer school at the University in 1938. The Federal agency heretofore mentioned has in its possession the testimony of two witnesses who corroborate Mr. Hewitt's statement that Professor Rader was in New York in the summer of 1938. All of this evidence has been made available to the proper state authority and has been made available to the administration of the University of Washington and the Board of Regents. When Mr. Hewitt informed your Committee that he recognized Rader as a former attendant of the Briehl school for Communist educators, your Chairman [Albert Canwell] immediately invited Professor Rader to his office. Professor Rader came into the executive office but as soon as he saw Hewitt, and before a word had been spoken, he turned on his heels, and said he refused to have any conversation. As Rader hurriedly left, Mr. Hewitt again identified him positively as the Mr. Rader that attended the Briehl school. Upon leaving the room Rader said he would not talk without his attorney. Your Chairman then courteously invited him to return with his attorney. Shortly thereafter, Attorney Ed. Henry, claiming to represent Professor Rader, showed up but Rader was not with him. Professor Rader would have had every opportunity, had he returned with Henry, to examine and cross-examine Hewitt, as did Henry. Hewitt persisted in his identification but Rader was not there to offer any denial."

"The fully authenticated and documented records of your Committee," Mr. Foley continued to read, showed

Professor Rader to have been associated with twelve organizations "officially cited as Communist Fronts and subversive. . . . Your Committee feels that the perjury charge against Mr. Hewitt was not only hasty and unwarranted but of political significance." The prosecutor of King County originally admitted that the perjury charge was invalid and agreed to seek a dismissal of the charge, but then reversed himself and explained that he was under promise to his predecessor (now a judge) not to do so, and that he might lose twelve thousand votes in the next election if the charge were thus dismissed.

Having finished reading the report of the committee, Mr. Foley expressed his own strong feelings in the matter. "If some witness were to testify that I attended a Communist School," he hotly asserted, "he would be personally confronted with me forthwith; and if he gave that testimony under oath, as was forecast by the Chairman, I would have him arrested as he left the stand. I would have that much interest in my good name, my reputation for patriotism and decency—all of which I would consider maligned by such an accusation." The contrary behavior of Rader was a straw that showed how the wind really blew. "There was no recrimination, there was no expression of indignation. It was taken in stride; and this offended man, who now seeks to bring this Relator three thousand miles to stand trial, allowed the matter to pass; he could not commit himself as to whether he was an American or a Communist until he had seen a lawyer. And his lawyer was present, he had his opportunity for examination, and although this Relator remained there several days, it was not until several weeks after he left the jurisdiction that they brought a proceeding which technically would make him a fugitive from justice."

There had been no indictment by a grand jury even after ten months. The only basis of the charge was the unsupported swearing of Mr. Rader. Aware of his duty and oath, having been district attorney for sixteen years, Mr. Foley affirmed that justice was the most important end of court procedures. He had signed thousands of extradition orders, but he did not feel that an essential showing could be made in favor of doing so in the present instance.

"I am aware of the limitations that are imposed upon me in arguing before your Honor, and this I put to you has not been intended or is intended to be an argument; nor does it go to the merits of the case specifically; nor do I intend to infringe upon any phase of this proceeding where I should be precluded by either ethics or rule from commenting. But I do think that instead of having it come before your Honor in the ordinary courts, where you would consider only technical and strictly legal aspects and their bearing upon the rights of this man, that I was in conscience bound to give you this outline, and let you sense my reaction to it." Acknowledging that this procedure was "technically irrelevant," the district attorney concluded that he had done what he felt morally bound to do.

Mr. Lee, the assistant district attorney, then rose and called for a return to the writ of habeas corpus. The return was duly made, and the warrant produced.

It was now the turn of Carl Rachlin, attorney for George Hewitt. "May it please the Court," he began, "the Honorable District Attorney has presented the facts in such an objective and eloquent way that there is very little that I can add or even attempt to add; and what I have to say will, before I make my motion to sustain the writ, be brief." He then asked permission of the court to put witnesses on the stand, and the court consented.

He first called upon George Hewitt, the Relator. After Hewitt was duly sworn and identified as living at 1750 Bronx Park East, Rachlin asked:

"You are the party who has testified in the State of Washington concerning Professor Melvin Rader?"

"Yes, sir."

"At this point I would like to show you a photograph," declared Mr. Rachlin, handing a picture to the witness. "Will you identify the person whose photograph that is, please."

"This is Professor Rader."

"Professor Melvin Rader who was mentioned by the Honorable District Attorney?"

"Yes, sir."

"All right; that is all."

The photograph was received in evidence as Relator's Exhibit 1. Mr. Rachlin then called his second witness, Mr. Manning Johnson, a dark and very tall Negro, who after he had been sworn in quickly identified himself as a resident at 492 Convent Avenue, New York City, and then explained that he had been not a Communist of the rank and file but a member of the National Committee. He was asked:

"Briefly will you describe what a member of the National Committee is?"

"A member of the National Committee is a person who holds one of the highest and one of the most responsible positions within the gift of the Party."

"Now at this point I would like to show you Relator's Exhibit No. 1, a photograph. Can you identify the first time you saw the person in the photograph?"

"Yes, I can identify him."

"Will you tell me where was the first time you saw the person in that photograph?"

"I first met him at the Communist Party Headquarters with Isidore Begun."

"Who is Isidore Begun?"

"Isidore Begun is a member of the Communist Party in the Educational Group."

"Do you remember what year you saw the person in that photograph?"

"That was in the year of 1938."

"And was this the National Headquarters of the Communist Party?"

"It was the National Headquarters of the Communist Party."

"And did you see that person at the National Headquarters of the Communist Party in 1938 on more than one occasion?"

"I saw him a number of times, going in and out of the office."

"Now, did you have occasion in the summer of 1938 to teach at this school previously referred to as Briehl's Farm?"

"Yes. I was sent there to deliver a lecture on the Communist position on the Negro question; and it was during the course of my lecturing that I had the occasion of seeing Professor Rader. He was one of the students in that class."

"No further questions, your Honor," concluded Mr. Rachlin.

Then Mr. Lee, the assistant district attorney, cross-examined Manning Johnson. In reply to questions, Johnson explained that Briehl's Farm was "a secret national school" maintained by the Communist Party. Educators were brought there for "special training" to promote "revolutionary work amongst the professors throughout the nation." "Only members of the Communist Party who were carefully screened and carefully selected were eligible for attendance." Pointing to the picture of Melvin Rader which Johnson held, Mr. Lee asked, "You are positive that picture you have there is a true representation of a man whom you saw at that school in the summer of 1938?" Johnson replied that he was positive.

"That's all," said Mr. Lee. Then Mr. Rachlin rose and called George Peters to the stand. He too was a Negro, short and very dark. In reply to questions he identified himself as living at 217 West 60th Street and having been a member of the Communist Party from 1933 to 1939. Shown the same photograph that Hewitt and Johnson had identified, he declared that he was "positive" that he had "seen that man before."

"Will you describe the circumstances of the first time that you saw him?"

Peters explained that in the summer of 1938 he had met Rader in the presence of George Hewitt. They had just emerged from some kind of meeting, and Rader excused himself, saying, "I am in a very big hurry." Later he had met Rader at Briehl's Farm. "I went up about the same month in 1938, around about August or September," he said, "I don't know exact what month [sic]; and I met this man Dr. Rader again."

"Did you see him more than once at that camp?"

"Yes, I did."

"To your knowledge were there any persons other than Communists attending this Briehl's Farm?"

"No."

[138]

After a brief cross-examination, in which the witness explained that he had visited Briehl's Farm on a two-day vacation, he was excused.

The time had come for Attorney Rachlin to make his plea. "Your Honor," he said, rising to his feet and addressing the judge, "it becomes incumbent upon me to express some opinions as to some of the other issues involved in this case. Firstly, I think it is important to tell the Court that George Hewitt is a married man, father of three children, and that there is a fourth one on its way. The reason I urge that is not for any mere sentimental reasons, although I think we should not ignore them, but because what is being asked in this case is that George Hewitt leave the State of New York, his home, and be sent three thousand miles away, on the mere sworn affidavit of a man whose word, to put it politely, is questionable, as has been mentioned by the Honorable District Attorney. . . . Mr. Hewitt will have to leave his family, if this Court sees fit to recognize the request from the State of Washington, and I think, and again it is no secret, his family will have to become a public charge upon the City and State of New York."

Hewitt, he went on to explain, was once a national committeeman of the Communist Party, and one of the most important Communists in the United States—so much so in fact that he was sent to Moscow to attend the Lenin School for Espionage, so that he could come back and prepare the way for the "Revolution." This fact, Mr. Rachlin explained to the court, is "perhaps the most important thing in the entire case"—since a man with this experience can be very helpful in exposing Communism. "He has left the Party, and has now helped the Department of Justice, helped the Grand Jury, helped various legislatures in their investigations of subversive activities. The Communist Party as a result feels that they must get rid of him. This is no idle talk on my part. I would like the privilege of showing to this court two copies of the *Daily Worker*."

"I don't want to look at it," interposed the judge.

"The items are on the front page," Mr. Rachlin explained.

"I don't want to see them, excuse me," said the judge.

"This is the type of case this is, your Honor," observed Mr. Rachlin. "There isn't much I can add to this. George Hewitt is as innocent as it is possible for a human being to be innocent."

"I never saw the *Daily Worker*," the judge persisted, "and I hope I never will."

Concluding, Mr. Rachlin moved that the writ of habeas corpus be sustained, and that the Relator be released from the custody of Detective Louis Hall and the state of New York.

Judge Levy then rendered his decision:

"Now let the Court declare itself for a brief moment or more, and say to this heroic District Attorney that it commends him most richly and most highly, not alone for a proper human acknowledgment of justice, but for the courage he has manifested in his attitude displayed at this hearing.

"It seems to me that a prosecuting attorney, as he well said, must not only concern himself with the proper prosecution of those guilty, but it is equally his concern to ascertain the innocence of people, if that be possible, in the orderly administration of true, genuine American justice.

"From what he has said and what I glean from these

reports, I learn that in the State of Washington there is any number of trained and iron-disciplined Communists who have operated with seeming immunity. Many of them hold almost impregnable positions of confidence and trust in their communities."

Turning again to the Report of the Committee to the Legislature, Judge Levy quoted at length to demonstrate that the state of Washington was riddled with Communists. But what stood out most conspicuously in the report, he observed, was that the prosecutor of King County, having admitted the validity of the evidence of Hewitt's guiltlessness and having definitely committed himself to seek dismissal of the perjury charge, later reversed himself and cynically explained that "it might cost him 12,000 votes when he runs for election to make such a step."

"I am wondering, really genuinely wondering," said the judge with emphasis, "what the civilization of that area is, when a public official charged with a very grave responsibility—the life and liberty of the members of his community—deigned to say that *votes*—never mind the number—would cause him to fail in his public duty. How long would such a prosecutor last in *this* civilization with utterances of that kind."

The court further remarked that the Canwell Committee had characterized Rader's attorneys as "unvarnished Communists." Having thus noted the quality of justice and the legal profession in the state of Washington, the judge concluded:

"There has not been made that showing which in good conscience I consider essential to warrant my sending this man to the State of Washington to eventual slaughter. If I were he, I would be very careful about my person. We have been told what happened to other men who were similarly situated.

"From these excerpts that I have presented—the District Attorney presenting them in part earlier—and from many things that are in these Reports to which the Legislature of the State of Washington has certified, I am convinced that this man committed no crime whatever; that if perjury was committed, it was committed by Melvin Rader, and that he ought to be the subject of a grand jury investigation rather than this accused; that the necessary requirements permitting extradition have not been established. And therefore this writ is sustained, and the prisoner is discharged."

"Thank you, your Honor," said Attorney Rachlin. The extradition hearing had ended.

12

The

Fight for

Exoneration

When Virginia and I read about the extradition hearing in the newspapers, the whole affair appeared to be as mad as the trial in *Alice in Wonderland*. Everything was reversed—right was wrong, truth was false. Instead of a genuine extradition hearing there was a bogus trial with the guilty side alone represented and the perjurer defended by perjurers. The "evidence" was legally inadmissible, no falsehood was challenged, and the decision was predetermined. Unlike Alice, I was not present to challenge injustice, but Judge Levy's looking-glass logic was as illogical as that of the Red Queen.

Even the *Seattle Post-Intelligencer*, inveterate defender of the Canwell Committee, criticized Judge Levy in an editorial: "It is doubtful if history records a more flagrant and gratuitous insult to the courts of one state from a court of another state than the remarks made by Supreme Court Justice Aaron Levy in New York this week. . . . It is all too true that the activities of certain citizens and certain former officials have given Washington an unenviable reputation in other sections of the country. But there is no justification whatever—and there never has been—for any intimation that the Washington judiciary has the slightest Communist contamination." The *Post-Intelligencer* did not make the more important point that the extradition hearing had been conducted in violation of constitutional requirements.

When I read the news of the hearing, I stated to the *Seattle Times:* "My family and I deeply resent the fact that a citizen with a long record of integrity can be subjected to malicious slander with no opportunity to clear his name in court. If the Un-American Activities Committee hearings last summer had been conducted democratically, with the right of the accused to cross-examine witnesses, this kind of attack upon me never would have occurred."

No criticism could alter the finality of Judge Levy's verdict. "This washes the whole thing up," Prosecutor Carroll told the *Post-Intelligencer.* "It's all over now." He made no attempt to appeal the decision, and I was powerless to do so. No official spoke out in my defense; the administration at the university remained silent. The evidence that Virginia and I had collected was unpublished, and the published evidence was all against me. So we continued to live under the stigma of Hewitt's accusations.

Thoughtful and informed conservatives were nevertheless puzzled by my case. They knew that Hewitt had been indicted for perjury under a reputable prosecuting attorney, that his successor in office had refused to dismiss the perjury indictment despite strong pressure to do so, and that the university administration, although its announced policy was to discharge Communists, had pressed no charges against me.

Soon after the extradition hearing, Managing Editor Russell McGrath of the *Seattle Times* called reporter Edwin O. Guthman into his office. "The courts have broken down," said McGrath. "Now it's our job to find out the truth." Ed Guthman hustled out of the city office with a long-term assignment.

He made an appointment by telephone and came out to our home. Dark, tall, and heavy-set, he was a thirty-year-old graduate of the University of Washington and a Purple Heart veteran of the Italian campaign in World War II. His broad grin looked boyish, but the grin disappeared when he talked about his assignment.

Although Grenafore Schneider had attended the extradition hearing and sent us detailed notes, Virginia and I had not seen the evidence that Guthman now presented to us. He had photostatic copies of the exhibits that had been introduced into the hearing—not only the affidavits of Manning Johnson and George Peters, which repeated in essence their testimony on the stand, but also the affidavits of Mrs. Quincy Mueller and Mrs. Ida Kirby, which flatly contradicted their statements to the King County Prosecuting Attorney and my sworn testimony before the Canwell Committee. There was also a photograph of Mrs. Mueller's index file card with the date "8–16–40," which apparently verified the contention of the Canwell Committee that August, 1940, was the time of our stay at the lodge. Guthman was obviously impressed by all this evidence.

It was necessary to convince him that the truth was on our side. We pointed out that the index file card bore our

1938 address, and that we had moved to a new address before the summer of 1939. We showed him the affidavits we had collected from persons who knew of our stay at Canyon Creek in the summer of 1938, and we told him about the records of the National Bank of Commerce, the University of Washington Library, the County Court House, and Dr. Carl Jensen the oculist. Taking nothing for granted, he checked every item. He drove up to Canyon Creek and interviewed Mrs. Mueller and Mrs. Kirby and the later proprietor of the lodge, Thomas Grant. He endeavored, without success, to track down the missing lodge register. Just as thoroughly he searched for all the evidence that might be used against me, checking the details of my political activities and interviewing Canwell more than once. But Canwell refused to give him permission to examine the committee's files and accused the *Times* of aiding the Communists.

His investigation was a matter not of days but of weeks. The spring lapsed into summer, and the *Times* remained silent. Virginia and I suspected that the editors, for reasons of politics or prudence, had decided against disclosing the facts. We consequently felt stymied. At this point I was approached by a new investigator, Vern Countryman, a young and slender professor of law from Yale University. He was one of a group of scholars who had received a grant from the Rockefeller Foundation to study the impact upon civil liberties of federal and state un-American activities committees and kindred agencies. When he interviewed me on August 5, I was struck by his intelligence and open-mindedness, and I gave him a full and candid account of the facts in my case. Like Guthman, he examined the whole body of evidence and confirmed its truth by interviewing all the principal witnesses and informants, including Canwell and his staff. Virginia and I were much heartened by the honesty and exhaustiveness of his investigations, but we realized it would be a long time before his findings could be published.

We wanted a public statement of exoneration from the university without delay. Since President Allen was in the East during the summer, I approached Dean Edwin Guthrie, the next in command. I asked that all my evidence be thoroughly reviewed, that Albert Canwell be asked to disclose *his* evidence, and that the university administration make public its conclusions. I confirmed this oral request in a letter dated August 19. "Since the charges against me are very serious," I wrote, "and since the question whether I have committed perjury is in issue, I feel that I have a personal right to have the evidence produced and evaluated. The interests of the University of Washington itself are at stake, for if the charges against me are true and I have committed perjury, I should of course be dismissed." There was no immediate reply.

Then something very surprising happened. I received an invitation from the Standard Oil Company of New Jersey to participate in a conference at Rockefeller Center in New York. The purpose of the "Jersey Roundtable," I was told, was to bring together university professors and company officials for an exchange of views. Altogether there would be about a dozen professors representing sundry institutions and fields of study, and all expenses would be paid by Standard Oil. I leaped at this opportunity to visit New York and participate in the Roundtable. While in the city I might discover more about Hewitt, Manning Johnson, and the extradition hearing. I even toyed with the idea of finding some way to publicize the truth through a national news medium. When I packed my luggage for the air flight I put in photostats, affidavits, and documents that proved the falsity of Hewitt's charges.

Since the Standard Oil Company was generous in its expense allowance, I had enough money to stay in New York not only for the duration of the Roundtable but for two weeks thereafter. The conference itself, high up in the great Esso skyscraper, continued until September 2, and I took a rather lively part in the discussions of social policy. When the conference was over, I moved from my hotel to the home of the Schneiders, at their kind invitation. During the remaining two weeks I explored New York, doing the many things that eager tourists undertake.

In the midst of all my other activities, I never forgot the Rader-Hewitt case. Even before the Jersey Roundtable concluded its sessions, I had begun to investigate. One of the guests at the conference was Harold Taylor, a philosopher from the University of Wisconsin who had recently been appointed president of Sarah Lawrence College. We agreed to eat lunch together, and he invited Matthew Radom, a personnel expert for Standard Oil, to join us. Both of these young men were inquisitive about the recent disturbances at the University of Washington, and they were amazed when I told them about the developments in my own case. They agreed that the remedy lay in publicizing the facts and were eager to help. Radom offered to arrange interviews for me with radio and newsmen and other people of influence. Taylor offered to introduce me to Freda Kirchwey, the editor of the *Nation*, and to speak to Morris Ernst and Arthur Garfield Hays, the famous liberal attorneys.

Even before the Jersey Roundtable Conference was over, Radom arranged an appointment with Sam Abelow, an official of the Columbia Broadcasting System, to discuss a possible program on my story. When I confronted Mr. Abelow in his office, I explained that an exposure of the facts in the Hewitt-Rader case might help to quiet the anti-Red hysteria and make it more difficult to trample upon American traditions of justice and fair play. I briefly summarized my evidence to indicate that it was incontrovertible. Mr. Abelow listened politely and said that he would take the question under advisement.

Through Taylor an appointment was arranged with officials at the office of the American Civil Liberties Union. When I reached the union headquarters with my briefcase bulging with evidence, I found that the staff counsel, a young man named Herbert Levy, was rather cool. He explained that officially the A.C.L.U. had taken no part in the defense of Hewitt, and that Carl Rachlin had acted as a private attorney. I was then ushered into the office of Roger Baldwin, the great man of the civil liberties movement. He was heavy-set and middle-aged, with a thoughtful and reassuring manner. Apparently impressed by the few items of evidence that I showed him, he suggested that I talk with Rachlin and Diamond, Hewitt's attorneys, and an appointment was arranged for the next day.

The conversation with the young attorneys—almost three hours long—took place in a room at the union headquarters. I spoke to them as a liberal like themselves, explained that the Canwell Committee had played a terribly illiberal role, and showed them enough evidence to convince any fair-minded person that Hewitt's testimony was false. They seemed to me decent men who, having been deceived by the apparently strong evidence in Hewitt's favor, were now embarrassed and on the defensive. At the end of our long conversation, they agreed that I should obtain a transcript of the extradition hearing and suggested that it might be possible to arrange for an A.C.L.U. lawyer to go with me to interview District Attorney Foley.

That interview never took place. Two days later I telephoned Levy, the staff counsel, and he replied that everybody in the union office was "too busy" to help me. With no one from the union to go along, I decided not to see either Foley or Judge Aaron Levy. I reasoned that, however innocent Rachlin must have been, the extradition hearing otherwise must have been "fixed," that the judge and the district attorney must have been parties to the fixing, and that I, as victim of their plotting, would be unwelcome. Now, as I look back, I regret that I did not see them. It would at least have been interesting to have observed their reaction.

In the meantime, Radom had got in touch with Governor Dewey's legal adviser, Charles Breitel, who agreed to discuss the Hewitt case with me. After a long train ride to Albany, I found Breitel, a polished gentleman, in his office in the old capitol building. In the course of our conversation, he stated that Governor Dewey had been subjected to heavy pressure not to issue the writ for Hewitt's arrest and extradition. I wondered whether it had been the Canwell Committee or the Department of Justice or both that had brought the pressure. What happened at the extradition hearing, Breitel said, was irregular, but he asserted that the responsibility rested with the district attorney and the court.

The day after I returned from Albany, I went to the

Bronx County Court House, where the extradition hearing had taken place, and hunted up the court reporter, Anna Pohlmann. She remembered the hearing, showed me the courtroom in which it had occurred, and promised to transcribe the testimony for a reasonable fee. Soon after I returned to Seattle, she sent me the transcript.

Before leaving New York, I considered what more might be done about exposing the facts to the public. Matt Radom had spoken to the liberal editor of *Collier's Magazine*, who appeared interested, and the journalist Joseph Alsop had suggested to author Helen Lynd, with whom I had recently corresponded, that either the *New Yorker* or *Harper's* might be receptive. But my attorney Paul Coughlin, hearing from Virginia that I was seeking publicity, wrote to me: "One difficulty about ordinary publicity by ordinary methods is that I am quite sure you will not be able to exercise any considerable measure of control over it and that it is likely to be sensational in tone. I think also that sensational charges on your behalf will be met by sensational charges from the other side." Half-convinced by this admonition, I decided to wait and see if the *Seattle Times* would break the story. Judging from a long-distance telephone conversation I had with Guthman, this might happen soon.

I felt that I had done all I could in New York, and after thanking Herbert and Grenafore Schneider for their hospitality, I caught a plane for Seattle early on the morning of September 16. Virginia and Lenore Forbes met me at the airport, and we all had an excellent dinner at our favorite restaurant, the Bohemian Café. I was soon back in the swing of things, taking the children to see the Pollack Brothers Circus and working on the final draft of my *Ethics and Society*. Meanwhile, unknown to me was the fact that both Ed Guthman and William Blethen, publisher of the *Times*, were trying to persuade Canwell to come to Seattle to explain what seemed to them strong evidence that I could not have attended the Communist school. Guthman tried to get him to come. He stalled. Blethen called him personally, and again Canwell stalled.

Awaiting me when I returned to my office was the long-delayed reply from Dean Guthrie to my letter of August 19. "I do not believe," wrote the dean, "that the University should, as you suggest, make demands on Mr. Canwell for materials in his possession. I think that under the circumstances that should be left to your own resources under the law. . . . In a legal sense the University is not an interested party." I then wrote again to Dean Guthrie pointing out that Canwell stated in his Report to the Legislature that he had already presented the evidence against me to the president and the Board of Regents. "Surely it is only fair," I said, "to ask that the contrary evidence be examined. . . . Since the charges against me are extremely serious, and since the evidence in my possession is conclusive, it is important that the real facts be known to you and the President in a manner that leaves no room for doubt."

This second letter brought a prompt response. President Allen's secretary informed me by telephone that the president and Dean Guthrie would like to review my evidence. The interview turned out to be decisive. When I had finished presenting the evidence, I asked the president to state publicly that the charges against me were false. He replied that he would ask Canwell to go over the evidence in my presence and, if he could not refute it, the president himself would express confidence in my innocence. Dr. Allen was true to his word, calling Canwell by telephone and giving him a week to come from Spokane to Seattle. Shortly thereafter Allen informed me that Canwell had agreed to the confrontation.

The time set for the showdown was October 20, but the day arrived and Canwell did not keep the appointment. The president, I suspect, called him again and "talked turkey"—at any rate he showed up in the president's office the next day. There I confronted him in a tense four-hour session. Either the president or his representative Don Anderson was present during the entire period.

My main purpose was to refute the charge that I had attended the Communist training school in New York State for a period of six weeks in the summer of 1938. Much of the evidence I submitted consisted of affidavits from persons who knew of our presence at Canyon Creek Lodge during that summer. Included were affidavits from Mrs. Angelo Pellegrini, who, accompanied by her husband and small daughter, drove us to Canyon Creek; Dr. Raymond Loy, who extracted Virginia's tooth in his office at nearby Granite Falls and who remembered that I was present; Louisa Petterson, Virginia's sister, who stayed in our home while we were at Canyon Creek; and Lucille Newman, Virginia's cousin, who recalled several corroborative details. The affidavits of Mrs. Quincy Mueller, the former owner of the Lodge, and Ida Kirby, the caretaker, corrected the misimpressions created by their original statements to the Canwell Committee investigators and corroborated my testimony. Among the other items of evidence were a withdrawal card from the University of Washington library bearing my signature and showing that I had borrowed a book on July 29, 1938; the office record of Dr. Carl Jensen that proved that I had had my eyes tested for glasses on August 15, 1938; the record of the Seattle city clerk that I had voted in the primary election on September 13, 1938; and records in the university comptroller's office that I had taught during the first session of summer school until July 20. Lest it be thought that I might have been at the Briehl's Farm school in the summer of 1939 or 1940, I submitted conclusive documentary evidence covering these two periods. None of the evidence I submitted was refuted, and no intelligent or fair-minded person could doubt it.

Canwell remained silent. At the end of the long session, when he was questioned by Ed Guthman and other newsmen, he was evasive and said nothing in my favor. "If Rader got a bad deal, it was as much his fault as ours," he declared, "and I'm not convinced he got a bad deal." I was furious when I heard these words. I turned my back and stared out of the window in an effort to control my temper.

President Allen promptly issued his statement of exoneration. Affirming his conviction that I had been falsely accused, he said among other things: "The University of Washington administration is fully satisfied by the present evidence that Mr. Hewitt's allegations have been disproved." Backing up the president's action, Judge Lloyd Shorett was explicit: "From my investigation when I was prosecuting attorney I am convinced that Rader never was a Communist; never attended the Communist summer school in 1938 or 1939; and that he was in Washington State during the time Hewitt said Rader attended the Communist school. I am convinced that Hewitt's testimony in this regard was false, and that the manner in which the New York court refused Hewitt's extradition was a disgrace to the administration of justice and the dignity of our courts." Fifteen months after Hewitt's original testimony, I was thus exonerated. It had been a long and hard ordeal.

Ed Guthman told the story under banner headlines in the *Seattle Times* of October 21. Among other details he explained the index card taken from the files of Canyon Creek Lodge. He quoted from an interview with Mrs. Quincy Mueller that the card was from an index she had used for correspondence purposes, and that the notation "8–16–40" on the card referred to the date on which she had written to Virginia and me in an effort to sell us a lot near the resort. The correct date of our stay at the lodge was indicated on the card by our 1938 address which, as the city's telephone books and directories proved, we left before the next summer. Guthman similarly debunked the other evidence that had been introduced into the extradition hearing.

His report, distinguished not only for its accuracy but for its human warmth and insight, was awarded the Pulitzer Prize for the best national reporting of 1949. The story, once told, was echoed by newspapers and magazines throughout the country.

I was deeply stirred by these events, not only because I was personally vindicated but because justice prevailed. As I stated to Guthman: "Thanks to the fact that I live in a democracy and that many people have helped me, I have been able to clear my name." In this one instance at least, misrepresentation and blind prejudice had been defeated by fair play and a free press.

13

The

Disappearing

Records

Despite Guthman's investigation, the mystery of the lodge register was still unresolved. The receipt for the register had been signed by investigator Aaron R. Coleman, and this receipt was in the hands of Thomas Grant, the present owner of the lodge. Ida Kirby had been present when one of the investigators had run his finger down a register page and remarked, "There it is—Rader—'38." This very crucial item of evidence—my signature dated in the summer of 1938—had thus been discovered by agents of the Un-American Activities Committee within three days after Hewitt concluded his testimony. Canwell and his staff, nevertheless, denied that they knew anything about the register, and the committee, in its official report to the legislature, declared that my *first* visit to the lodge was two years after the date of my 1938 signature.

At the conclusion of the four-hour session in President

Allen's office, Canwell was questioned by reporters as to what had happened to the register. He said he could not remember whether he had ever seen it or whether his committee investigators had ever taken it from the lodge. When asked if he would be willing to assist in a search of the committee's files to see if it might be there, he snapped: "It is not my job. If Professor Rader or anyone else thinks the register will do him some good, let him look for it."

The Canwell Committee had thus apparently suppressed documentary evidence that I had told the truth and Hewitt had lied. To have concealed this evidence when Hewitt was under indictment for perjury was itself a crime. Two statutes from the criminal code of the state of Washington were pertinent:

"Section 2362. Destroying evidence. Every person who, with intent to conceal the commission of any felony, or to protect or conceal the identity of any person committing the same, or with intent to delay or hinder the administration of the law or to prevent the production thereof at any time, in any court or before any officer, tribunal, judge or magistrate, shall willfully destroy, alter, erase, obliterate *or conceal* any book, paper, record, writing, instrument or thing, shall be guilty of a gross misdemeanor" (my italics).

"Section 2347. Injury to the public record. Every person who shall willfully and unlawfully remove, alter, mutilate, destroy, *conceal* or obliterate a record, map, book, paper, document or other thing filed or deposited in a public office, or with any public officer, by authority of law, shall be punished by imprisonment in the state penitentiary for not more than five years, or by a fine of not more than one thousand dollars, or by both" (my italics).

Section 2362 obviously applied in the present instance, and Section 2347 would be applicable if the register had ever been deposited in the office of the committee. Investigator Coleman had admitted to Vern Countryman that he had removed records from the lodge and had deposited them in the committee's office, although he denied any knowledge that the pages from the register were among these records, or that there was anything in them to show that I was at the lodge in 1938. From a secretary in the committee's office Guthman had elicited the information that the register had been received and deposited there. Neither Countryman nor Guthman publicly disclosed this information.

A week after President Allen issued his statement of exoneration, State Attorney General Smith Troy agreed to investigate the apparent suppression of evidence. "The indication that public records may have been suppressed raises a very serious question," declared Troy in the *Seattle Times;* ". . . this question is of national importance. It is above politics." State Senator Lester T. Parker, Republican president pro tempore of the senate, and Representative Charles W. Hodde, Democratic speaker of the house, were chosen to assist Troy. Charles Carroll requested that the results of the investigation be reported to the prosecutor's office.

After four months of investigation Troy announced that Canwell Committee investigators had taken register pages bearing my name from Canyon Creek Lodge, that these pages had not been located, and that he intended to ask the president of the senate and the speaker of the house to open and search the committee's locked files. Canwell replied that opening the files would be a "calamity" which would aid the Communists, that the register was not in the files, and that he thought he knew where it was. The legislative council then gave Canwell ten days to produce the register and appointed a committee of three council members to search the files if he should fail to do so.

Faced by this ultimatum, Canwell declared in the Spokane *Spokesman-Review* on April 20, 1950: "The missing register was never of sufficient importance to cause us to look for it. Other evidence presented by Professor Rader made it clear that he could not have been in New York City in the summer of 1938, as had been charged by a witness against him. And actually we had no evidence that Rader had been a Communist except the so-far unsupported testimony of that one witness." To mitigate the effect of this statement he added: "But we did have definite evidence of Rader's connection with a number of Communist-front groups. . . ." Thus Canwell, while lamely excusing the suppression of the register and continuing to press the Communist-front charges, finally admitted that the principal charge against me was false.

Three days later on April 23, 1950, Canwell delivered a stack of loose-leaf pages from the register to Prosecutor Carroll. The pages contained signatures and addresses, some followed by dates and some not. At the bottom of one page were Virginia's and my undated signatures. These were the signatures for our visit in June when we had gone to reconnoiter and to make reservations for later in the summer. The last dated signature preceding our names on that page was June 12, 1938, and we must have signed the same day or shortly thereafter. The pages for the first week in August—the week when we registered a second time—were missing. These pages may have been removed and destroyed. Nothing would have been easier than to delete one or more of the loose-leaf pages.

Even without the later signature, the facts were damning enough. The committee investigators had picked up the register. If it had shown that I had not been at Canyon Creek Lodge when I said I was, then the committee most certainly would have brought it forward as Exhibit A. But if the register supported my account, then the committee had reason to conceal it, and of course they did exactly that.

In a letter to Carroll printed in the *Post-Intelligencer*, Canwell declared that my June signature on the register could "offer no conclusive proof in establishing whether or not Professor Rader attended the Briehl Communist School in New York in the summer of 1938." He neglected to remark that my signature contradicted the statement in his report to the State Legislature that I first visited the lodge in 1940. Also he did not satisfactorily explain why this evidence had been suppressed for twenty-one months. The article in the *Post-Intelligencer* written by Fred Niendorff, the principal champion of the Canwell Committee in the public press, left the impression that Hewitt's charges might well be true, and that my associations with subversive organizations had been substantial.

The next day Guthman disclosed in the *Times* two new items of evidence. The first had been supplied by Mrs. Mueller. Searching through her Canyon Creek records for notes pertaining to a business transaction, she found the lodge rent receipt book for the summer of 1938. An entry in this book read: "Rader, paid to September 5, 1938—$20." The second item was a letter from Frank Ketchum, who had been the cabin boy during our stay at the lodge, and who was now living in Yakima, Washington. After explaining that he had been a lodge employee in August, 1938, he wrote: "Now, as to that Professor

Rader, yes, I remember him. Now if he was a Red he was very different from any I ever ran across. And as for him being in New York at any time during that month, that was impossible. I used to take wood and kindling to them regularly."

Two weeks later on May 5, Smith Troy released his report. It confirmed not only that the page with our 1938 signatures had been carried away from the lodge, but that "all the records" taken from the resort "were delivered to the committee headquarters in Seattle." These records, "which should have been stored in the locked room with the balance of the files," had mysteriously disappeared. "All committee investigators were asked if they had the records in their possession . . . and all answered in the negative save Stith, who said to our investigators, 'I refuse to say Yes or No to that question.' " The pages of the register which Canwell "belatedly delivered" to Prosecutor Carroll "conclusively prove," said Troy, "that the Raders were at the Lodge in 1938, and that their first appearance was not in 1940 as stated in the report to the Legislature." Although Troy noted that the registrations for the first week in August were still missing, he said there was no doubt that we had been at Canyon Creek during that month. He mentioned, among other items of evidence, that all the women at the lodge who had observed Virginia noted that she was pregnant and that the birth certificate of Barbara Rader indicated that the date of conception was around May 15, 1938. This meant that the pregnancy would not have been noticeable by June 12 but would have been apparent in August. Troy remarked, "This is nature's testimony and not the kind of evidence that could be fabricated by an alibi." He concluded that the total body of evidence proves "beyond doubt that

Melvin Rader was at Canyon Creek Lodge during the period fixed by George Hewitt as the time he swears he saw Rader at the Briehl School for Communists in New York State."

The events that I have narrated were bound to have political repercussions. "Communist Fighter Al Canwell," as he characterized himself in his campaign literature, had hoped to climb to high political office through his fame as committee chairman. In 1950 he sought the Republican nomination to oppose United States Senator Warren Magnuson but was defeated in the primary election. Running for congressman-at-large on the Republican ticket in 1952 and 1954, he lost both times to the Democratic candidate, Don Magnuson. Most of the members of his committee fared no better when they sought re-election.

In its final report to the State Legislature in January, 1949, the committee had listed among its achievements the accumulation of "an index file of approximately 40,000 subjects dealing with Communists, their Front Organizations and activities and related materials." To safeguard these precious records, armed members of the Washington State Patrol carried three safes from the committee's Seattle headquarters to the Legislative Building in Olympia and placed them in a locked room. The keys to this room were then put in a safe-deposit vault which was not to be opened unless the president of the senate and the speaker of the house were present and so authorized. The three safes, supposedly containing voluminous records, remained locked for six years.

Finally in February, 1955, the State Legislature voted to turn over the files to the Federal Bureau of Investigation. In the presence of the speaker of the house, the president of the senate, the lieutenant governor, and two representatives of the F.B.I., the room was unlocked. Since the combination for only one of the safes was known, a safe expert was called to crack open the others. To the consternation of everyone present, two of the safes yielded only a few dusty papers and books, and the remaining safe was empty!

The House of Representatives then voted unanimously to investigate the mystery of the missing records, and Canwell was subpoenaed to appear on February 21. When questioned on the stand in the packed hearing room, he admitted that he had destroyed a large portion of the records. He destroyed them, he said, to protect his sources of information and to prevent them from falling into the wrong hands.

"Much of the reports went through the fireplace of my home," he testified. "Nobody said how long we should keep them. They were for our own use."

"Do you feel the Legislature set you up in business to the tune of $140,000 for your own personal use?" demanded House Speaker John L. O'Brien.*

"No, sir," Canwell replied, "for the State of Washington."

"Did you set yourself up as the sole judge of what was to be done with the records?" O'Brien asked.

"Precisely, yes, sir," responded Canwell. "I was discharging a high responsibility, and there are people in this Legislature who should appreciate that I destroyed these records."

"That's where we differ," said O'Brien.

When Canwell testified that some of the records had

---

* The Speaker's estimate was too low. The Canwell Committee spent approximately $158,000 of the taxpayers' money.

been microfilmed, he was asked what had happened to the microfilm.

"I decline to answer," said Canwell.

When pressed for an answer, he said the microfilm "might be in the hands of an agency whose business is not public."

"Did you give it to the F.B.I.?" asked O'Brien.

"I decline to answer."*

"Are you asking immunity under the Fifth Amendment?"

"No, only Communists do that."

*When Canwell refused to answer whether he had given microfilms to the F.B.I., the State Legislature in its 1955 session passed House Concurrent Resolution No. 5 retroactively authorizing the transfer of Canwell Committee records to the Bureau. The Resolution was a bipartisan attempt to prevent the Canwell affair from again becoming a hot issue. In the winter and spring of 1968, Assistant United States Attorney John Darrah had occasion repeatedly to visit the locked storage room of the F.B.I. in the basement of the Federal Reserve Building in Seattle. He noticed a large box labeled "Canwell Committee" on a high shelf. Having been informed of this discovery, Richard C. Berner, head of the archives division of the University of Washington library, informed Darrah that he would like to obtain the records for permanent storage in the state archives. Accordingly Darrah contacted J. Earl Milnes, special agent in charge of the Seattle office of the F.B.I., requesting the release of the records to the state archives. Milnes said he could give no quick answer, but asked Darrah to write him a formal request. Darrah wrote the letter but received no reply. Finally in 1975 he again approached the Bureau and repeated the request. In a written reply dated July 23, 1975, Philip T. Basher, Special Agent in Charge, reported: "These records have been destroyed in accordance with Federal regulations pertaining to the destruction of records collected and maintained by the Federal Bureau of Investigation." As Darrah, who is the source of the above information, wrote: "It is truly sad that after more than twenty years of elapsed time the Bureau could not recognize the importance of these papers as historical documents" (letter to James M. Dolliver, Administrative Assistant to Governor Daniel J. Evans, December 1, 1975).

"Do you wish to be in contempt of the Legislature?"

"I'm not in contempt of the Legislature."

All that Canwell would say was that he did not have the microfilm, and he refused to give an explanation.

The question of the missing records has never been resolved. Canwell was not cited for contempt, nor was he prosecuted under Section 2347 of the Criminal Code for injury or destruction of the public records; but the taxpaying public took note.

Down to the time of Canwell's testimony (February 21, 1955) the ghost of the Canwell Committee still flitted about. At every session of the State Legislature there was a determined effort to revive the committee under a new chairmanship. In 1949 the State Senate passed a bill introduced by R. L. Rutter and Harold G. Kimball, members of the old committee, to extend its life. But the Democratic majority in the house adopted an alternative bill to transfer the committee's functions to the attorney general and the legislative council with procedural safeguards for persons being investigated, including the opportunity to cross-examine accusing witnesses and submit rebuttal evidence. Each branch of the legislature refused to accept the other's bill, and when the senate tried to establish its own exclusive committee the move was blocked by the attorney general, who issued an opinion, based on state constitutional law, that no single body of the legislature can legally create an interim committee to function after legislative adjournment. Again in 1951 the effort to revive the Committee on Un-American Activities ended in a stalemate between the two houses, and in later sessions attempts to resuscitate the committee were even less successful. Finally its ghost was laid low by Canwell's testimony just cited.

14

The

Okanogan

Trial

THE Canwell Committee no longer haunted us, but Al Canwell himself was active. After his political defeats, he established the "American Intelligence Service" in Spokane, a city of about 180,000 in eastern Washington. As part of this service he maintained a bookstore stocked with John Birch Society publications and a "Freedom Library" devoted to "pro-American and anti-Communist" books, pamphlets, and taped speeches and interviews. He also kept files on hundreds of persons alleged to have links with Communism and distributed selected items of "information" through his newsletter, the *Vigilante*. On the wall above his desk hung pictures of former Senators Joseph R. McCarthy and William Jenner.

Although he lived in eastern Washington, he noted what was happening on the western side of the mountains. When a storm of controversy broke out over a widely exhibited filmstrip, *Communism on the Map*, he leaped into the fray. Remarking that the University of Washington had not been spared the "infection of communism," he questioned the motives of ninety-two faculty members who signed a press statement criticizing the film for its "irresponsible mingling of fact and falsehood." "Because the University of Washington is located within the strategic invasion path from Russia," Canwell told his audiences, "great efforts have been made by Reds to colonize it—and with considerable success."

Such forays received little notice in the news media, but late in 1963 and early in 1964 Canwell was exposed to the full glare of publicity during the famous Goldmark libel suit. No novel or play could have made the issues more clear and dramatic. The liberals and their right-wing enemies faced each other in grim antagonism. Each side was determined, and in ten weeks of trial there was not one gesture of compromise. The contest took place in an old courthouse in the little town of Okanogan in eastern Washington. The defendants were Canwell and three right-wing associates. One of these was Ashley Holden, who had been an ardent supporter of the Canwell Committee when he was political writer for Spokane's newspaper, the *Spokesman Review*. More recently as editor and owner of a country newspaper, the *Tonasket Tribune*, he had cooperated with Canwell in the dissemination of the American Intelligence Service reports. The two other defendants were John Caron, a state organizer for the John Birch Society, and Loris Gillespie, a member of the society and wealthy orchardist. Pitted against these men were John Goldmark and his wife Sally.

Goldmark, who was forty-six years old at the time of the trial, had served three terms as representative of the Okanogan region in the Washington State Legislature, where he had risen to the chairmanship of the House Ways and Means Committee. He had been elected in 1956, 1958, and 1960 by three-to-two margins, but he was defeated three-to-one in the 1964 primary campaign on the issue of "Communism." The libel suit was filed by Mr. and Mrs. Goldmark two weeks after the primary. According to their brief, they had been "systematically charged . . . with being Communists, Communist agents, Communist sympathizers, and members of Communist front organizations, all for the purpose of convincing the people of Okanogan and Douglas Counties that plaintiffs are subversive and are disloyal to the Government of the United States." The attack by the defendants had been by word of mouth, newspaper articles and editorials, leaflets distributed by mail or by hand, and taped speeches and interviews played before anti-Communist study groups. Canwell and his colleagues were charged with having used these means falsely to blacken the reputation of the Goldmarks.

The wording of the complaint might erroneously suggest that John and Sally Goldmark had been equally the targets of the libel campaign. In fact John was the target, not Sally. The main defendants—Canwell, Holden, and Gillespie—had known of Sally's past membership in the Communist Party for about five years. An employee of the House Committee on Un-American Activities had leaked the story to Canwell in 1956, but his associates did not disclose the information at that time, having apparently decided to save it for an opportune moment. Finally the upward surge of the right wing in 1961 inspired them to undertake an all-out assault upon John Goldmark, at first by inciting local Democratic Party leaders to turn against him. When this maneuver failed (thanks largely to a steadfast Democratic county chairman), they began a long series of public attacks in which John was the target. Sally's past Communist Party membership was primarily a means of indicting him.

In bringing suit, Goldmark's attorneys wrestled with the touchy question how best to handle the fact of Sally's past Communist Party membership, which the Goldmarks had never announced to the voters. Wishing to minimize public prejudice, they decided that the best course was to "get out in front on this issue." For this reason, they asked damages for Sally in a lesser amount on two of the six counts of libel. Their aim was to place her past squarely before the public, to prove that she had left the Party long ago, and to show that they were not ashamed of her record. Except for this decision, Sally would not have been a plaintiff at all.

The story of the marathon trial is worth a book in itself. There were more than a hundred witnesses, and their testimony ran to thousands of pages in the court reporter's transcript. I shall limit myself to salient aspects that are relevant to my narrative. Although the main focus of the trial was the relation of the defendants to the Goldmarks, I was unexpectedly swept into the fray—old charges were revived, a new charge was hurled against me, and I was forced to be a witness. I was involved because there were many references during the testimony to the old Canwell Committee hearing and because the American Civil Liberties Union was, in a sense, "on trial." During the election campaign of 1962, Canwell and Holden seized upon the fact that Goldmark was a member of the state advisory board of the union. In articles in the *Tonasket Tribune*, Holden characterized the A.C.L.U. as "an organization closely affiliated with the Communist movement in the United States" and called Goldmark "a tool of a monstrous conspiracy to remake America into a totalitarian state." At a stormy meeting sponsored by the American Legion, Canwell described the union as "the major Communist front operating in the State of Washington at the present time" and damned Goldmark as one of its leaders. These attacks were among the principal counts in the libel suit. At the time of trial I had been recently president of the Washington division of the A.C.L.U., and the defense conceived the plan of attacking the union by reviving the old charges against me. This strategy, they hoped, would also serve to rehabilitate the reputation of Canwell, whose committee had been criticized earlier in the trial for its handling of my case.

For more than a decade I had been active in the union. During much of this time I was a member of the state board of directors, and in 1957 and again in 1962–63 I served as president. My decision to join the union was motivated largely by my reaction to the Canwell Committee and the extradition hearing. Not only did I resent the injury to my family and myself inflicted by the committee —I objected on principle to its policies and tactics. When I discovered that the American Civil Liberties Union was dedicated to the counterprinciples of fair play and free expression, I was immediately attracted.

Unwittingly, the Canwell Committee had performed a great service to me as an individual, since it forced me to recast my basic political convictions. In the period of the Depression, I felt that the ideal of human equality must take precedence over every other ideal, so great was the disparity between rich and poor and so urgent was the problem of want. To this ideal of equality the more sincere Communists were devoted, and to this they were prepared to sacrifice the ideal of liberty. After my experiences with the Canwell Committee, I continued to believe intensely in human equality, but freedom seemed to me no less paramount. I realized that both the radicals who believe in equality to the neglect of liberty, and the liberals who believe in liberty to the neglect of equality, have a one-sided view of the world. The ultrarightists are even more mistaken, since they care little or not at all for either value.

I joined the American Civil Liberties Union because I hate totalitarianism in any form and because the union helps to create a liberal and militant public opinion without which the best constitution in the world is a mere scrap of paper. During my second term as president of the state of Washington branch, our attorneys carried to the United States Supreme Court the fight against a repressive loyalty oath imposed upon all public school teachers and a similar oath required of all other state employees. On June 1, 1964, the verdict was rendered. Mr. Justice White, speaking for the majority of seven to two, declared the Washington State loyalty oaths unconstitutional. Among the consequences of this historical precedent was the striking down of oaths in state after state. In Arizona, Maryland, New York, Oregon, Georgia, Colorado, Pennsylvania, Texas, New Hampshire, Massachusetts, Nebraska, California, and other states, oaths have recently been challenged or struck down. As a member of the union and one of the plaintiffs in the original case, I shared in the deep satisfaction of this victory.

Although the decision of the United States Supreme Court in our favor was not rendered until after the Okanogan trial, the action of the A.C.L.U. in bringing the suit had already been widely publicized. I had been not only an officer in the union but one of the plaintiffs when this case was pressed.

Neither understanding nor caring for the constitutional principles at stake, the far right could see in our suit only a rejection of the concept of loyalty. A great many of the other actions of the American Civil Liberties Union have been interpreted by extreme conservatives as subversive. The union believes that civil liberties are for *all* Americans, and defends the constitutional rights of Communists, American Nazis, Ku Klux Klansmen, Jehovah's Witnesses, Black Muslims, nudists, free lovers, and unpopular individuals and groups of every kind. The union almost never finds itself defending the rights of a popular organization, such as the Boy Scouts or the Red Cross, because these groups have ordinarily no difficulty in exercising their constitutional rights. Since the public too seldom understands the distinction between holding an unpopular view and defending the right of someone else to hold it, the American Civil Liberties Union has incurred intense hostility and has often been called a Communist front. It had been thus characterized by Canwell and Holden in their attacks upon John Goldmark.

As I have explained, the defense in the Okanogan trial hoped to show, by attacking me, that the Civil Liberties Union in Washington State was under subversive leadership. The instrument for carrying out this strategy was Barbara Hartle, who had been a member of the Communist Party for twenty-one years and former organizational secretary of the Party in the Northwest District. For conspiring to overthrow the government of the United States, she had been convicted and sentenced to the federal penitentiary in 1953 under the Smith Act. While still a convict she repudiated the Party and appeared in Seattle as a "friendly witness" before the House Committee on Un-American Activities in 1954, testifying for about five days and identifying several hundreds of persons whom she had allegedly known as Communists. She thereafter received "executive clemency" and was released from prison "for her valuable assistance to the Justice Department of the United States." Subsequently she testified on numerous occasions in committee hearings, deportation or denaturalization cases, and Smith Act proceedings.

In interrogating Mrs. Hartle during the trial, defense attorney E. Glenn Harmon finally broached the question of my alleged Communist activities. When the plaintiffs' attorney William Dwyer objected, Harmon explained to the court that the question whether Canwell and his committee had falsely charged me with being a member of the Communist Party had been raised by the plaintiffs and was an issue in the case. He also pointed out that Melvin Rader was a member of the board and past president of the Washington Civil Liberties Union. The judge overruled Dwyer's objection primarily on the basis of the A.C.L.U. issue.

"What are the facts as to whether Mr. Rader was under Communist Party discipline?" asked Harmon.

"I knew him to be under Communist Party discipline," replied Mrs. Hartle. "He was known to be a member of the Communist Party."

Under Dwyer's cross-examination, she testified that, in the winter of 1936–37 or 1937–38, she had attended a small Communist group meeting in the Ballard or Interbay district of Seattle and that I was present. She said she could remember the names of only two others who were there—Professor Herbert Phillips and the wife of a university faculty member whose name I shall not repeat.

(When I obtained this information I telephoned the latter, and she vehemently denied the charge.)

When Mrs. Hartle was asked how she could identify the individuals present as Communist Party members, she replied, "Well, I was told that this was a Communist meeting."

"Did Mr. Rader say anything?"

"I don't recall that he did."

Dwyer then reminded her that she had named a great many persons as former or present Communists in her testimony before the House Committee on Un-American Activities in its 1954 Seattle hearing.

"I think there were several hundred names . . . ," she admitted.

"Would about five hundred be right?" asked Dwyer.

"Well, I don't know, I never counted the names. It seems a little high."

Dwyer pointed out that she had not named "Professor Rader."

"I don't think I did," she replied.

"You don't have any doubt about it, do you?"

"No, I don't as far as I recall now. . . ."

Dwyer then produced an indexed transcript of her 1954 testimony, and after examining the transcript Mrs. Hartle agreed that I was not among those named.

These details of the cross-examination did not appear in the Seattle newspapers. All I knew was that the charge of "Communism" had been hurled at me afresh and trumpeted through the news media. I issued a sharp denial to the press. "So far as I know, I have never met the woman in my life," I said. "I have never been a member of the Communist Party. I have never been under Communist Party discipline."

Mrs. Hartle testified in mid-December, but I had to wait until the defense had completed its case in early January before I could appear as a rebuttal witness. On Tuesday, January 7, I caught a bus to Okanogan and arrived late in the afternoon, registering at the hotel. During the next day I sat in the courtroom and watched reactions among the spectators. It was not difficult to pick out partisans for one side or the other. The community was so sharply divided that I wondered whether the jury would be able to agree upon a verdict. John Goldmark and his attorneys were grouped around one large table, and the defendants and their attorneys around another. I instantly recognized Al Canwell, who looked much older than when I first met him. Beside him were Ashley Holden, with tidy mustache and gray hair, and the other two defendants. Among several defense lawyers, Glenn Harmon from Spokane—a portly man with heavy-rimmed spectacles—did the cross-examining on the days when I was there. At the table reserved for the prosecution sat William Dwyer, a young lawyer whom I knew from past associations in the American Civil Liberties Union, and beside him were his co-counsel, middle-aged R. E. Mansfield of Okanogan, and John Goldmark, appearing more youthful than his forty-six years. Later I met Mrs. Goldmark, a distinguished-looking woman with stylish clothes and dignified manner.

It was not until Thursday afternoon, January 9, that I was called to the stand by Dwyer. I was more tense and emotional that I had expected to be. The old wounds were deep, and they had been reopened by this new testimony.

Dwyer's questions and my answers were brief. I testified that I had never been a Communist, had never attended a closed meeting of the Communist Party, had never been under Communist Party discipline, and, so far as I knew, had never met Barbara Hartle.

In cross-examination, Attorney Harmon questioned me about my participation in United Front organizations, such as the Congress against War and Fascism. I answered as I had in 1948 to similar questions before the Canwell Committee. The court adjourned for the day before the cross-examination was completed.

The next morning Harmon returned to the attack, but I had regained my composure. Again and again he sought to implicate me in subversive activities. Since his questions were of the sort that I had answered during the Canwell Committee hearing in 1948, I shall not go over this old ground again.

Finally Harmon referred to what I had said in my book *No Compromise*, which had earlier been a matter of controversy during the Canwell Committee hearing. "Isn't it a fact," he demanded, "that you classed Soviet Russia as a democracy?"

"It is not a fact; that is false," I replied.

". . . Did you class Soviet Russia at all? Did you class it as totalitarian?"

When I wrote the book, I explained, the Soviet Union was opposed to Hitler and, to this extent, on the side of the democracies; but in September, 1939, after the Nazi-Soviet Pact had been signed, I wrote an introduction for the British edition in which I stated unequivocally that America "cannot" and "should not be neutral as between the Allied Powers and the opposing powers."

"I want to point out," I said emphatically, "that this was directly contrary to the Communist line at the time. The Communist line . . . right after the Soviet-German pact was that we ought to be neutral and I was saying the exact contrary of that. And if there is any doubt about it, I happen to have a copy of that book in my hotel room and I will go and produce it."

I had brought a copy of the British edition with me to Okanogan, thinking that I might wish to refer to it, but Harmon showed no inclination to accept my challenge.

"Let's see," asked Harmon, "you are a member and Past President of the Washington Chapter of the American Civil Liberties Union, aren't you?"

"I am very proud to say so."

"It is true, is it not, Professor Rader, that while you were President of the State American Civil Liberties Union you were bitterly opposed to teaching any courses in the public schools of this state which would include material derogatory to the Soviet Russia brand of Communism?"

"That is not at all true."

"I would like to make an offer of proof, Your Honor," said Harmon addressing the judge.

"I would like to have the opportunity of rebuttal," I interposed.

Judge Turner, suppressing a smile, cautioned me, "Your function here is simply to answer questions."

Harmon was referring to a meeting of a citizens' advisory committee called together by the State Superintendent of Public Instruction, Louis Bruno, in Olympia, September 27, 1961. At this meeting in the state capitol, the subject of discussion was the question whether teaching about Americanism, Communism, or both was a proper responsibility of the public schools, and if so, by what methods should the teaching be conducted. The liberals present opposed the establishment of a compulsory course in anti-Communism, and inserted in the committee's report a recommendation urging the rejection of "propaganda techniques," and "the development in all courses of the spirit of inquiry and the skills of critical thinking." As the representative of the American Civil Liberties Union, I took part in the very spirited debate. Pleading for academic freedom, I found myself personally attacked by Mr. Paul Stoffel, editor of an eastern Washington newspaper, the *Pullman Herald*. His charges were subsequently spelled out in detail in editorials in his newspaper on October 5 and November 2, 1961. Citing the Canwell Committee investigation and Hewitt's testimony against me, Stoffel charged that I had been active in thirteen "Communist front" organizations and that I had never, to his knowledge, taken a stand contrary to the Communist Party line. He also clearly implied that I was a master of deceit.

The strangest of all his accusations was that I had brought to the Olympia meeting "two persons who evidently shared [my] views that nothing derogatory of Communism should be taught in the schools." One of the two persons to whom he evidently referred was Edwin T. Pratt, the young Negro executive director of the Seattle Urban League, who happened to sit down beside me and with whom I later had lunch. It was the first and only time that I ever conversed with Pratt, but in the light of later events I shall never forget the occasion. Pratt dedicated his life to the fight for human equality, and like others who believed in human brotherhood, he fell before an assassin. On January 26, 1969, he was murdered in the doorway of his home, struck in the face at close range with a shotgun slug.

To return to my main narrative, Harmon evidently had

been in communication with Stoffel or someone like him, and wished to revive the attack upon me. But Judge Turner, in private session during a recess, ruled that a review of these old charges would be an unwarranted proliferation of issues.

After Harmon had finished the cross-examination, Dwyer asked me how I happened to "join some organizations in the 1930's that had a number of Communists in them."

I replied: "This was a time of deep depression when there were a good many millions unemployed and desperate poverty on the part of a great many people who were losing their farms and their homes. It was also a time when Hitler and Mussolini and the Japanese Fascists were very much on the march, and there was a great movement toward a world war. Under these circumstances it seemed to me that it was extremely important to unite and to try to prevent war. These organizations were dedicated to this purpose. They were extremely active in pursuing the purpose of . . . stopping Hitler and the other Fascists while there was still time. I believed that if there could be enough unity in the world to do these things that then the world would be spared an immense amount of suffering. That is why I went into these organizations."

Dwyer asked me why I had never been a Communist. "I think that dialectical materialism is a crude and dogmatic philosophy," I answered. "As an American, I believe in the Bill of Rights, in the fundamental constitutional liberties and human rights written into our Constitution—and I don't believe the Communists believe that and respect that. Also I think that the Communist theory is very lopsided in its emphasis upon economic causes. That seems to me a very great misreading of history. Those are the basic reasons."

Before I was excused from the witness stand, I noticed that Ed Guthman had entered the room and taken a seat among the audience. He was no longer the fledgling reporter I had known in 1948–49, but his sturdy build and black hair still gave him a youthful appearance.

Mrs. Hartle was recalled and questioned briefly. I looked at her closely, trying to remember whether I had ever seen her before. She was a short and pinched-looking woman about my own age. Perhaps I had met her at a United Front gathering in the thirties. That was so long ago that I could not be sure.

Dwyer asked: "Mrs. Hartle, in the year of 1954, during the time that you were a witness before the House Un-American Activities Committee in Seattle, did you tell Mr. Ed Guthman—Edwin Guthman—in a conversation between you and him that Melvin Rader had never been a Communist or a member of the Communist Party; that you knew that the Communist Party had tried to get him to join on several occasions, but that you also knew that their efforts had always met with failure?"

"No, I did not."

"That is all, Your Honor," said Dwyer.

Guthman was then called to the stand and interrogated. He testified that he was presently employed in the Department of Justice as chief press assistant to Attorney General Robert Kennedy. Then he explained that during the year 1948 he had covered the Canwell Committee hearings as a reporter for the *Seattle Times*, and that he had subsequently investigated my case and written about it.

"After your articles appeared," Dwyer asked, "did you

or did you not remain interested in the dispute concerning Professor Rader?"

"I did," he said, remarking that in the 1950's he had made an effort to talk about me with people who were then in the process of leaving the Communist Party.

"Was Mrs. Hartle one such person?"

"Yes, she was," replied Guthman.

He was then asked when and where the interrogation had occurred and what was said.

"I covered the House Un-American Activities Committee hearings at which Mrs. Hartle testified, 1954 and 1956," he answered. "My recollection is that in 1954 I asked her during a recess whether Professor Rader had ever been a member of the Communist Party. I recall that she answered to me that he had not been; that they had sought to recruit him into the Communist Party and that he had refused to join."

"Did she indicate whether or not they had attempted more than once to get him to join the Communist Party?" he was asked.

"It is my recollection that she said that they had tried on numerous occasions to recruit him into the Communist Party."

"How clear or how certain are you about this conversation with Mrs. Hartle?"

"I am *very* clear," Guthman replied with emphasis.

Under Harmon's cross-examination he stood his ground. "I have a very clear recollection that the conversation took place," he reiterated, "and a very clear recollection of what was said."

Harmon asked him why he did not write a newspaper story about the conversation. "As a matter of fact," Harmon insisted, "it was quite a news story, wasn't it?"

[181]

"What, Mr. Harmon?"

"On verification . . . that Mr. Rader in fact was not a member of the Communist Party at the time he was accused, wasn't that a news story?"

"No, it wasn't."

Harmon's voice rose, he pounded the table in front of him. "Mr. Guthman," he snapped, "I was a newspaper man for ten years, and isn't it a fact that that was a scoop of the first water?"

"I can only tell you, Mr. Harmon, what I did."

Guthman explained that the *Seattle Times* had printed the essential facts in 1949, and that the statements of Mrs. Hartle in 1954 merely duplicated what had already been published.

"And it was not a news story?" Harmon doggedly persisted.

"Well, I didn't write it."

"Yes, I know you didn't write it, but did it happen?"

"Certainly it happened."

That afternoon Guthman and I flew to Seattle in a private plane used to transport the plaintiffs' witnesses to and from Okanogan. It was a clear day, and the mountains lay below us in their sparkling majesty. As we gazed down upon the snowy peaks and the rolling wooded ravines, we discussed the moral degradation of former Communists who stooped to perjury. We agreed that such persons as George Hewitt, Manning Johnson, and Barbara Hartle could not be understood as solitary individuals. While still Communists they had been instructed by the Party that the end justifies the means, and they retained this belief when they switched sides. They belonged to an "age of informers" just as Canwell and his committee belonged to an "era of McCarthyism." There had been similar or worse maladies in other times and places—for example, the excesses among the Greeks during the Peloponnesian War, the hysteria among anti-Catholics during the time of Titus Oates, the Palmer raids in the United States toward the end of World War I, and the terrible abuses under Stalin and Hitler. In such periods of hot and cold war, hate is uninhibited and scruples are cast to the winds.

Guthman and I also discussed the assassination of President John F. Kennedy and the reactions of Robert Kennedy and Lyndon Johnson. The murder of the President had occurred while the Okanogan trial was in full swing, and the little drama in the old courthouse somehow appeared connected with these great events. The defendants had tried to exploit the tragedy by treating it as proof of the "internal Communist menace," but the relation between the trial and Kennedy's death was more subtle and profound than that. Guthman and I felt that both events indicated a deep disquiet and malaise in our social order. The bullet that tore a hole through Kennedy's head also tore a deep wound in the soul of America. Little did we guess that Martin Luther King and Robert Kennedy, among others, would soon fall before the assassins' bullets. The murders, riots, violent demonstrations, and acrimonious disputes during the ensuing Johnson administration revealed how angrily the country had turned in upon itself. But the Okanogan trial exposed the anger that was already there, ready to be whipped into fury.

So far I have dwelt upon my own involvement in the Okanogan trial, but the testimony of its principal figures, the Goldmarks and their accusers, was of course far more central to the case. Both John and Sally Goldmark testified at length. She told why she had long ago joined and left the Communist Party, making clear that she regretted her early mistake, and denying the defense's charge that she had been mixed up with espionage. John testified that he had never been connected with the Party or a member of a Communist front. The campaign against him, he asserted, was a revival of the old McCarthy tactics: "Label your opponents as Communists in order to discredit them." Asked what he had done to fight Communism, he replied: "I have done the most I can do to support . . . the development of the United States as a free country in which political discussions can be carried on without hatred or suspicion."

Typical of the defense was the testimony of Canwell. He told about the operation of his private intelligence service and testified as an expert on subversive activities. As an "expert" he asserted that the National Council of Churches was Communist infiltrated and reiterated his charge that the American Civil Liberties Union was a Communist front. Listing various actions of the Goldmarks, such as their opposition to the House Committee on Un-American Activities, he concluded: "All of these things and many others add up to an observation in my mind that they are, have been and are still today, under Communist Party discipline."

To back up Canwell and his associates, the defense called to the stand other "experts": Donald Jackson, a former California congressman who had served for years on the House Committee on Un-American Activities; Herbert Philbrick, counterspy and author of the best-selling book, *I Was a Communist for the F.B.I.*; and John Lautner and Karl Prussion, former members of the Communist Party and frequent witnesses at trials and hearings. They all sought to indict John Goldmark for allegedly following the Communist line and to pillory Sally Goldmark as a former Communist. The plaintiffs also mobilized a formidable array of witnesses, including former United States Senator Harry Cain, who had served three years on the Subversive Activities Control Board under President Eisenhower; John Pemberton, the national director of the American Civil Liberties Union; Paul Jacobs, a well-known political writer and expert on labor unions and Communism; and Sterling Hayden, the Hollywood actor, who had recently taken a leading role in the motion picture *Dr. Strangelove*, and whose experiences as a former member of the Communist Party were closely parallel with Sally Goldmark's.

In the last week of the trial, the lawyers made their final arguments. Speaking for the prosecution, William Dwyer declared: "We are here and we have spent all this time and taken this segment out of our lives for the simple reason that a man's good name has been attacked, destroyed, vilified, dragged through the mud, not once, not twice, but practically every day for a period that is now going on to be two years." In a very detailed review of the evidence, Dwyer castigated the defendants and their witnesses for constructing "a web of lies and conjectures and miserably sordid, unhappy speculation about the motives and ideas and beliefs of people whom they don't even know and about whom they don't care." In concluding he asked the jury: "Is this country still the country that we have always thought it was where people can move to a community and settle down and do their best to earn the respect of their fellow citizens and be judged for what they are and what they do? . . . Or have we become so afraid and so terrified of the world and the Communist threat that we are now willing to turn upon each other out of fear and hatred and in the process destroy the very freedoms which our country has been built on, which we have always cherished and which are the real reason that we choose to live here rather than somewhere else? That is the broader question in the case and your verdict, I think, will supply the answer to it."

Although Glenn Harmon made a lengthy plea, gray-haired Joseph Wicks, former Okanogan judge, was the most dramatic of the defense counsel. He strode about the courtroom and pointed and gesticulated. "This enemy of ours, Communism, is like a dog infected with rabies—a mad dog—turned loose in the world," he shouted. "It has bitten and infected some of our own people." Citing the First Commandment, "Thou shalt have no other God before me," he cried: "Now, would a Communist accept that? What is God to an atheistic Communist?" At this point Mrs. Goldmark, a sincerely religious woman, burst into tears and fled from the courtroom.

"Your verdict in this case," Wicks intoned, "will either be a signal to the most radical elements of our land to press harder to destroy the things that are in their way and to turn this land of ours into a welfare state, then into a socialist state and eventually into a state of Communism —or your verdict will be an announcement to the world that in this little valley of Okanogan we still believe as free men, God-fearing American citizens. . . . It shouldn't take long, Ladies and Gentlemen, to decide the issues. And when you return with a verdict for these defendants on every count claimed in this case, you will sound a clarion that will ring through the corridors of this old courthouse. It will shake the dome of the capitol building at Olympia. It will reverberate through the halls of Congress . . . yes, it will be heard half way around the world, even in the Kremlin. . . . Then they will know that they cannot—that they must not and they shall not use the people to further a Godless ideology of Communism in this land of ours."

In responding for the prosecution, Mansfield said: "It will be my hope to restore to this courtroom a measure of reality. . . . Emotionalism does nothing toward the establishment of facts." He then reminded the jury of the real question at issue: "This case is not about the loss of an election. . . . This case is not about the Communist Party, although that is what the defendants would have you believe. . . . What this case is about is that people have been libelled. . . . The days of witch hunts in Old Salem are still with us."

After receiving lengthy instructions from Judge Theodore S. Turner, the jurors retired and deliberated for four and one half days. Mostly farmers, sawmill workers, and ranch wives, they were representative of the Okanogan country. When they were finally polled, they awarded John Goldmark $40,000 in damages—a whopping sum for a rural jury to pin on the defendants. It was larger than any libel award that had ever been affirmed in the history of the state of Washington. On every count involving the American Civil Liberties Union—the issue that had dragged me into the case—the damages awarded were substantial.

The verdict was widely hailed as a victory for liberalism and good sense. The *Portland Oregonian* declared in an editorial: "A few more verdicts like the one in Okanogan might restore the nation to a tolerant level where the constitutional freedoms could be exercised as they should be in a free country." And the *Washington Post* said: "The jury listened, learned, deliberated and rendered a just and thoughtful verdict—a vindication not alone for the Goldmarks but for the jury system and for democracy as well."

Then something quite unexpected happened. The United States Supreme Court, in the case of *New York Times* versus *Sullivan*, declared on March 9, 1964, that debate in an election campaign "should be uninhibited, robust and wide open," that "erroneous statement is inevitable in a free debate," and that "constitutional guarantees require . . . a federal rule that prohibits a public official from recovering damages for a defamatory falsehood relating to his official conduct unless he proves that the statement was made with 'actual malice.' " Since Goldmark was a public official at the time he was libeled, the Supreme Court ruling applied to his case. Taking account of the Supreme Court's decision, Judge Turner ruled that "factual errors" had been proven by the plaintiffs but "actual malice" had not, and that the state therefore lacked constitutional power to penalize the libelers.

In deciding whether to appeal to a higher court, the plaintiffs considered the uncertainty and high cost of litigation and the difficulty of collecting substantial monetary judgment. They decided not to appeal mainly because the Goldmarks' principal objective—vindication—had been attained. The judge's ruling in no way affected the jury's determination that the charges were false and libelous, and this was what the Goldmarks had undertaken to prove. Nothing could alter the fact that the jury had found in favor of the plaintiffs after reviewing all the pertinent evidence. This verdict reflected the considered judgment of a representative panel of American citizens. In a classic test of political extremism, they had decided in favor of justice and sanity. Canwell had long since been rejected by the electorate—now he had been repudiated by a jury of his peers.

In a real sense, the intrusion of the *New York Times* case represented a further liberal victory. The American Civil Liberties Union had urged such an outcome as *amicus curiae* ("friend of the court") before the Supreme Court, and the new ruling safeguarded free speech from punitive libel suits designed to stifle it. A great many such suits, arising from the racial issue, were then pending in the South.

15

Epilogue

MORE than five years have gone by since the end of the Okanogan trial and more than twenty years since the Canwell Committee hearing—yet these events have been etched so vividly in my memory that they seem "only yesterday." I look at the present with a kind of double vision: behind the New Left I see the Old Left, behind the Far Right of today I see the Extreme Right of twenty years ago.

The Okanogan trial, partial victory though it was, left me with a heavy heart. It disclosed a deep rift in American life—a rift that seemed to be widening as the forces of reaction gathered for the campaign of 1964. The cold warriors had stirred anew the bitter dregs of hatred.

Accusations against me, which I thought had long ago been laid to rest, had been revived as part of a larger pattern of events. On the witness stand Barbara Hartle testified that she had been a witness at trials, committee hearings, and deportation and denaturalization proceedings "fifteen to twenty-five times" (too often to count with accuracy!), labeling hundreds of persons as "subversive." Like the other "expert" defense witnesses in the trial, Herbert Philbrick, John Lautner, and Karl Prussion, she was a professional informer. I could not help wondering how many times she and her ilk had committed perjury.

The figures of the other perjurers, George Hewitt and Manning Johnson, rose up in my mind. In the months and years since the extradition hearing, I had learned a good deal more about them. Hewitt resumed work as consultant and witness for the Department of Justice as soon as his arrest was lifted. Suddenly in the summer of 1949 he collapsed while testifying in Cleveland during the Balint deportation case and was rushed to Bellevue Hospital in New York. The New York *Daily Compass*, in an article by the famous reporter I. F. Stone, disclosed on December 2, 1949, that Hewitt was confined in the neurological ward for a condition diagnosed as aphasia (a disease of speech and memory impairment caused either by a brain lesion or by a functional disorder). In January, 1950, he was released from the hospital after five and a half months' treatment. "He couldn't talk for a long time, but he's some better now," Mrs. Hewitt told an Associated Press reporter. "Sometimes he can't remember things. Some people tried to say he was in a 'psycho ward,' but that's not true. He just had a bad stroke. It also affected his heart." The improvement in Hewitt's condition was temporary.

When I heard the news of his death I recalled the signs of nervous disorder during his testimony before the Canwell Committee. I remembered his gibberish when he was asked why he had left the Communist Party and the symptoms of paranoia when he told how he was persecuted. I was appalled that a man so unbalanced had been employed by the Justice Department to send other men to prison. He had been used to oust Carl Marzani, formerly an economics instructor at New York University, from the Department of State, and to condemn him to a federal penitentiary. The case was so questionable that the United States Supreme Court, after twice hearing the arguments on appeal, split four to four. (The rule is that the court, on a tie vote, upholds the lower court; hence Marzani went to prison.)

Manning Johnson had a long and lucrative career as a professional witness. This career continued after he had been fully exposed as a perjurer by Ed Guthman in his Pulitzer Prize-winning articles and by Vern Countryman in his heavily documented book. While thousands of others were being thrown out of their jobs on the slightest suspicion of disloyalty, Johnson continued undisturbed. Employed by the Immigration and Naturalization Service of the Department of Justice, he testified in more than twenty-five court cases and before loyalty boards, Congressional hearings, and state un-American activities committees, including the Canwell Committee in the Pension Union hearing. On May 24–25, 1954, in a closed loyalty board probe, he was the principal accuser of Ralph Bunche, the Nobel Prize winner and high official of the United Nations Secretariat. The six-member board unanimously concluded that there was "no doubt" about Bunche's loyalty and recommended to the Department of Justice that Johnson be investigated for perjury. To its great discredit the department continued to employ him.

Finally, in a majority decision delivered by Mr. Justice Frankfurter on April 30, 1956, the United States Supreme Court ordered the rehearing of a case before the Subversive Activities Control Board because of false testimony by Manning Johnson and two other professional witnesses. According to the court, these men "have committed perjury, are completely untrustworthy and should be given no credence. . . . Because their character as professional perjurers has now been conclusively and publicly demonstrated, the Attorney General has ceased to employ any of them as witnesses." No longer employable by the government, Johnson wrote and spoke for the John Birch Society until his death a few years later. The society still distributes his pamphlet, *Color, Communism and Common Sense*, as an attack upon the civil rights movement. In this pamphlet George Hewitt is described as a martyr "driven to an untimely grave" by Communist persecution.

When I considered these three perjurers, George Hewitt, Manning Johnson, and Barbara Hartle, I was impressed by their leading roles on both sides in the Cold War. They had risen to high positions in the Communist hierarchy, and, after switching sides, they exposed their old comrades and lied about me and perhaps many others. Their conduct was shocking in itself, but more shocking was the use of such informers by the Justice Department.

This behavior can be understood only in the context of the Cold War. If men think in terms of a life-and-death conflict between the Communist and the Western worlds, each side is prone to cast the other into the stereotype of a monster. Then both sides act toward the other in ways that confirm their reciprocal image: they arm to the hilt, engage in mutual recriminations, and hunt down "subversives." The informer is prized, and the accused, not the accuser, must bear the burden of proof. In an ordinary courtroom there is considerable protection against injustice, but in a legislative hearing, or its Communist counterpart, the rules of evidence are suspended. Hence it becomes a haven for slander and perjury.

What happens in a single country is part of the world scene. Ours has been an age when one great crisis after another has plagued mankind. We have witnessed two world wars, the profoundest of all depressions, revolutionary movements of great scope and fury, and mounting civil strife. The twentieth century has been bloodier than all previous centuries put together, but our hyperbolic wars are petty in comparison with a future thermonuclear holocaust. Long before the bomb was dropped on Hiroshima, Freud in *Civilization and Its Discontents* warned us of our peril: "Men have gained control over the forces of nature to such an extent that with their help they would have no difficulty exterminating one another to the last man. They know this, and hence comes a long part of their current unrest, their unhappiness and their mood of anxiety." Freud's words have lost none of their force.

During a period of severe tensions men tend to lose their grip on freedom and tolerance. In a crisis situation there is nothing harder to bear than ambiguity, and frightened men are likely to think in black and white terms. There is a kind of historical law at work here—the law that tolerance is characteristic of a period of security and intolerance of insecurity. The events set forth in my narrative illustrate the truth of this law. The fists and stones of militants and the excesses of the police provide contemporary examples. At the same time, hotheads on both sides of the Cold War are pushing us toward the terminal catastrophe. It is to resist such hotheads that I have written the present book.

Justice William O. Douglas, in *The Anatomy of Liberty*, has phrased the main point that I wish to urge: "As the wife of an American Ambassador in Southeast Asia recently said to me, 'There is too much we-ness versus they-ness in the world. We are the "good"; they are the "bad"; just like cats are "good" and mice are "bad." We need to educate ourselves to the oneness of mankind.' . . . The concept of 'the good and bad,' 'we and they,' that has dominated the human race from the beginning, spells doomsday when projected into the nuclear age."

Carl Schmitt, a German political theorist, has argued that the "we and they" antithesis is the basis of all politics. His book, *Der Begriff des Politischen* (1933), begins with the declaration: "The essential political distinction is that between *friend* and *foe*. It gives to human actions and motives their political significance. All political motives and actions can be traced back ultimately to this distinction." Just as ethics is concerned with right and wrong, esthetics with beauty and ugliness, and economics with utility and disutility, so politics is concerned with the contrast between friend and enemy. This notion, I fear, leads straight to that colossal suicide-murder in which not only our enemies and ourselves but most of mankind will go up in smoke.

I reject this conception of politics, and I ask myself, will the time ever come when men will say "We" instead of "We and They"? Will we regard men of other nations and races and creeds as friends rather than as enemies? Will the great powers, Communist and non-Communist, learn to live together in peace and amity?

In reading and rereading the transcripts of the Canwell Committee hearing and the Okanogan trial, I have been struck by how constantly the rightists employ the rhetoric

[195]

of "We and They" and think in terms of friend and enemy. From their perspective, they are the loyal Americans, and those who oppose them, both liberals and radicals, are the subversives. Their favorite phrase is "the Communist conspiracy," and they apparently believe that the liberals are among the chief plotters. They cling, as so many have in the past, to a conspiracy theory of history. For the Inquisition, the conspirators were the Protestants; for Titus Oates and his followers, they were the Catholics; for the Nazis, they were the Jews; for the Communists, they were the capitalists and imperialists; and for the ultraright, they are the Communists and "fellow-travelers."

Nothing could be simpler, from the standpoint of intellectual effort and political sloganeering, than to trace all contemporary revolutions and most civil disturbances to "the Communist conspiracy" and to suppose that the goal of the conspirators is to overthrow the American government and all non-Communist states. The proponents of this interpretation condemn with undiscriminating fervor reforms and revolutions throughout the world. There is a neurotic and even a paranoid element in this concept of a worldwide malevolent conspiracy against which loyal Americans must wage an unremitting crusade.

I do not assert that conspiracies never happen or that Communists never conspire. But I do assert that the picture of a uniformly conspiratorial and ecumenical Communism is a dangerous mirage. Communist conspiracy is not nearly so common, successful, or monolithic as the rightists suppose.

The assumption that Communism is the sole cause of revolutionary ferment is very wide of the mark. If every Communist on earth should obligingly commit suicide, there would still be a great deal of revolutionary ferment. The world's unrest is caused by poverty, disease, injustice, and oppression—without these, agitation would fall upon deaf ears. The concept of monolithic Communism is equally false. We are in the presence of a variety of communisms; they are often at strife with one another; and the predominant tendency among them is nationalistic and polycentric. There is increasing pressure for moderation and independence within the Communist states themselves. When the Russian rulers respond by erecting the Berlin wall, or crushing the Hungarian revolt, or rolling their tanks into Czechoslovakia, they sow discontent among their own people and weaken their prestige and influence throughout the world. Finally, a supposition that Communists, socialists, and liberals all belong in the same pot is the most fantastic of all. It is exemplified in the indiscriminate slanders and perjuries of "friendly witnesses" before committees on un-American activities and similar bodies.

The tragedy is that the Red bogey has infected not only the irrational right but the mass of Americans as well. Without the common belief that Communism is on the march for the conquest of the world, we would not have supported the Bay of Pigs invasion, we would not have rushed our marines into Santo Domingo, we would not have tolerated the cloak-and-dagger methods of the Central Intelligence Agency, we would not have poured more bombs on little Viet Nam than we rained on all of Europe or Asia in World War II, we would not have permitted the growth of a military machine so huge that it has drained off the funds needed desperately to feed the hungry and fight urban decay, and we would not have supplied arms to eighty nations—no less!—to prop up, in many instances, antidemocratic dictatorships hypocritically classified as part of the Free World.

What is the truth about Communism? There is no short and simple answer. Marx stated, in his *Economic and Philosophical Manuscripts*, that Communism might take a raw and tyrannical form. "This entirely crude and repressive system," he declared, "would negate the personality of man in every sphere. . . . It would be a system in which universal envy sets itself up as a power, and . . . in this form of envy, it would reduce everything to a common level. . . . Crude Communism is only the culmination of such envy and leveling down to a preconceived minimum." He spoke of it as "the negation of the whole world of culture and civilization." One can imagine that much in Russia, China, and other Communist states would strike him unfavorably.

Marx predicted that class antagonisms would become ever more intensified as capitalism develops, and that the main spearhead of the revolution would be the revolt of militant industrial workers in the most mature capitalist countries. In sober fact, organized labor in capitalist America is nonrevolutionary; Communist revolution has broken out in relatively nonindustrialized countries such as Czarist Russia and China; and new revolutionary disturbances appear most likely in the industrially backward areas. Major "trouble spots," such as the Congo, Viet Nam, the Arab countries, and the restless Latin American states, fall within these underdeveloped regions. The impact of advanced technology upon predemocratized and preindustrialized countries has upset the world's applecart. When the sick, hungry, illiterate, and oppressed people of the "backward countries" see a possible end to their hideous misery, they are shaken out of their ancient torpor and respond with feverish zeal. Their revolutionary leaders, unconsciously exhibiting their own backward mentality, distort Marxism to fit conditions in these primitive societies. The Communism of Stalin, Mao, or Castro bears little resemblance to Marx's original version. It represents not so much the ideal of the future as the undertow of the past.

In the course of the Okanogan trial I was asked why I had never joined the Communist Party, and I replied that its dialectical materialism is too dogmatic, its attitude toward the Bill of Rights too disrespectful, and its emphasis upon economic causes too exclusive. All of these objections apply in some measure to the original content of Marxism, but they apply much more fully to the crude distortions of official Communist doctrine. As the writings of Marx become more fully known, a clearer comprehension of him as a profound and serious thinker is emerging. His features bear a strong resemblance to those of the humanists and existentialists of our own time.

Marx himself was aware of the tendency among "Marxists" to distort his ideas. "One thing I know," he said, "and that is that I am not a Marxist." Such distortion is illustrated in the "Marxist" conspiracy theory of history. I have already referred to this doctrine that wars and other social calamities are the result of a conspiracy on the part of capitalists and imperialists. Marx maintained no such doctrine. He contended that employee and employer alike are caught up in the net of impersonal economic forces, and that the capitalists, far from being master conspirators, are ruled by the blind forces of history which will inexorably bring on their ruin and disappearance as a class.

There are many divergent ideas and movements among

contemporary Marxists, and some of these we should heartily welcome. For example, consider an exchange of views on February 18, 1965, at an international convocation to examine the implications of the encyclical *Pacem in Terris* of Pope John XXIII. Under the auspices of the Center for the Study of Democratic Institutions, a gathering of religious, political, and intellectual leaders of all denominations and parties at New York's Hotel Hilton discussed the Pope's great admonition: "There is an immense task incumbent on all men of good will, namely, the task of restoring the relations of the human family in truth, in justice, in love, and in freedom." The famous American diplomat and authority on Communism, George F. Kennan, was among those who responded. He said that we need trust, honesty, and compassion to bring peace to the world. Each side should change to accommodate itself to the truth in the opposing view.

In his peroration he declared: "I should like . . . to end these observations with a plea for something resembling a new act of faith in the ultimate humanity and sobriety of the people on the other side; and I would like to address this plea to our communist contemporaries as well as ourselves. History reveals that the penalties for overcynicism in the estimation of the motives of others can be no smaller, on occasion, than the penalties for naivety. In the case at hand, I suppose that they may be even greater. For in the predication of only the worst motives on the adversary's part there lies, today, no hope at all: only a continued exacerbation of mutual tensions and the indefinite proliferation of nuclear weaponry." In the spirit of these remarks, he called for mutual trust and forbearance and the refusal to engage in senseless acts of destruction. "The act of faith that this requires," he concluded, "is something we must learn to see not only as the assumption of new risks to ourselves but as perhaps the only means whereby wholly intolerable risks could be avoided. Only in this way do we have a hope of approaching that state of mutual trust in international affairs which, in the words of the encyclical, 'is something which reason requires . . . and is eminently desirable in itself, and . . . will prove to be the source of many benefits.' "

Immediately after Kennan finished speaking a distinguished Communist philosopher from Poland, Adam Schaff, sprang to his feet. "I have no paper prepared," he exclaimed. "If I had one, I would reject it after what I have just heard. . . ." He began with "a confession" that he had come to the convocation "from a very different philosophical creed" from that of the encyclical or of the nonsocialist democracy that Kennan represented. "We have different evaluations as to the aims and goals of humanity, as to what human happiness means, as to which ways lead most directly toward this happiness. . . . But does this mean that we cannot do anything at all, that there is a fatality of stresses and fights, and that there cannot be progress? Not at all. . . . It means that none of us has a monopoly on truth and that all of us can learn from the writings and teachings of others. . . . Coexistence is a fight, a competition, a noble competition for the hearts and minds of people. This will continue, but let us hope that our conduct will be rational. On your side you will go further and further in expanding your economy, increasing social security, and so on, not only because you recognize that this is the normal course of development but because there is pressure from the socialist countries. On our side we are rapidly changing our political situation, bringing in more and more democracy, liberalizing the internal life of our society. This is also the normal course of development, but it is also the result of competition from you. We are coming closer and closer, and this is the great hope." There have been retrogressions in Poland since this statement was made, but it seems likely that in the long run liberalization will prevail.

I rejoice in such indications of good will and plead for an end to recrimination and hatred. It would be a glorious transformation if both sides could renounce hot and cold wars and devote their immense resources to constructive purposes. This kind of transformation has occurred before in history. At one time the Christian and Islamic peoples were locked in mortal combat, and both sides declaimed that no compromise was possible. Later the Catholics and Protestants were bitterly antagonistic. In both instances, the two sides found ways of peaceful coexistence—and the gain was of immeasurable magnitude. The conflict between Communism and anti-Communism, in its intensity and rancor, is akin to these religious wars of the past. Just as they were renounced, so may this latter-day conflict be. There is far more reason now to seek peace than ever in the past, since the hellish fury of scientific warfare has infinitely multiplied the danger.

The defeatists among us will say that war is such an ancient and entrenched institution that it can never be abolished. That is what men used to say about chattel slavery, but it was overthrown when it outlived its rationale. Many an ancient institution, such as feudalism, primogeniture, and the divine right of kings, has crumbled when it became anachronistic. Nothing could be more irrational, nothing more anachronistic, than militarism in this atomic age. No nation can win and every nation may perish in thermonuclear war. The human will to survival may forever revolt against this threat of universal death.

We can take heart in the deep revulsion against war that is spreading among young people all over the world. The extreme unpopularity of the Viet Nam war has been only one sign among many. There has been an increasing outcry against the exploitation of backward peoples and races; against the poverty which breeds violence; against rampant and embattled nationalism; against profit-making in military goods; against military training and classified research on the campus; against police violence in defense of the status quo; and against the whole ideology and rhetoric of "We and They."

The young have often antagonized their elders by their brashness and intemperance, but they have also brought fresh hope and vigor to the struggle for a better world. We can deeply sympathize with their demand for justice and equal opportunity for the blacks and other disadvantaged minorities. We can admire their determination to make education more relevant to the life-or-death-issues of this century. We can applaud their desire for revisions and reforms in the educational process and for meaningful participation in its planning and direction. We can join in their strong protest against the bureaucratization and alienation of man, recognizing that it is this mechanization of life, perhaps more than any other factor, that explains the worldwide revolt of youth. We can see in their cry for "participatory democracy" and grass-roots initiatives a wholesome protest against the disease of over-centralization—that apoplexy at the center and anemia at the extremities which afflicts brontisaurian organizations.

On all of these issues we should lend the students strong support, but we should not necessarily back everything they do and say. As a matter of principle and not mere expediency, I do not believe in the kind of hostile confrontation in which victory goes to whichever side can mobilize the most force. Although I deplore intransigence on both sides, I recognize that the students are responding to a deep malaise at the taproots of society, and that, in many instances, they are also reacting to the intemperance and inflexibility of those in authority. The new insight that we need is a grasp of the world's crisis in its depth and complexity and a realistic agenda of what to do about it.

We civilized human beings have fathomed many of the secrets of the universe; we have tapped the primal energies of nature; we have invented the mechanical means to wipe out poverty and to build a world community; but we have attained no corresponding cultivation of feeling and no adequate spiritual assimilation of the new ideas and techniques. The values and institutions of the free community have in no way kept pace with this revolutionary transformation. Power has increased so fast and so much; harmony has improved so slowly and so little. The price humanity has paid for this lag is manifest; it includes world wars, totalitarian regimes, class and racial tensions, anxiety and alienation everywhere spreading, and the possibility of nuclear Armageddon. Here, as nearly as one can sum it up in a few words, is the essence of the colossal crisis facing twentieth-century man.

The further question is what can be done. This is a question not so much for the men of my generation as for the young people who are taking our place, but the experience of us older liberals may be relevant to the tasks that lie ahead. We have lived through a longer span of history and should have attained a little wisdom. I think we can discern three main stages in our mental journey. The first stage was reached in the thirties when the Depression and Nazi-Fascist terror imperiled civilization. Then it appeared that human equality was the most pressing goal of mankind. In this period many of us enlisted in the United Front and some even joined the Communist Party. The second stage was reached in the late forties and the fifties when loyalty boards and un-American activities committees were rampant. The excesses of the inquisitors made us realize that liberty is no less precious than equality. These two stages I have dealt with in detail in the preceding chapters.

Now we are in the midst of the third and final stage. It came home to me as I listened to the angry overtones of the Okanogan trial and recoiled with a strong sense of the need for a viable community. It came home to millions of Americans through the murder of Medgar Evers, John F. Kennedy, Martin Luther King, Robert Kennedy, or, closer home, Edwin T. Pratt. The mass violence of urban riots and police bludgeonings has swept city after city, and every crime from murder to mayhem has stalked our streets. Our military machine has grown out of all proportion and has subjected a small underprivileged nation to the horror of napalm and saturation bombing. In the thirties there was far more hunger but much less violence than there is in the late sixties. To this extent, we Americans have retrogressed alarmingly.

We have thus come to appreciate, stage by stage, the three great watchwords of the French Revolution—equality, liberty, fraternity. Democracy can be defined as the harmonious combination of all three. Those who find nothing fresh and dynamic in the democratic ideal should ponder the words of Walt Whitman in *Democratic Vistas:* "We have frequently printed the word Democracy.

Yet I cannot too often repeat that it is a word the real gist of which sleeps, quite unawakened, notwithstanding the resonance and the many angry tempests out of which its syllables have come, from pen and tongue. It is a great word, whose history, I suppose, remains unwritten, because that history has yet to be enacted." Its history is unenacted because it calls for a transformation more profound than the world has ever seen.

This fact should fill us with hope rather than despair. Democracy, we dare to believe, will be achieved in forms which we cannot yet envisage and in a measure we cannot imagine. But to say that it is *wholly* unenacted is to exaggerate. Its accomplishments within the time span of my narrative have been considerable. There has been an immense change for the better since the dark days of the Depression and Nazi-Fascist tyranny. We tend to absorb the successes and take them for granted in our preoccupation with the failures. Looking far ahead, we have every reason to hope that democratic forces will carry the civil rights and antipoverty campaigns to victory, and that the mounting protest against war will finally prevail. There may be new political and social inventions that will humanize civilization and convert "the great society" into an open and friendly society. The growing sense of the importance of human rights is an earnest of things to come. Democracy can achieve the better life that humanity is demanding if it is sufficiently resolute.

On the other hand, we have seen the dreadful results of Fascist and Communist totalitarianism. There is no good reason to suppose that the dictatorship of the New Left, or even "the democratic educational dictatorship of free men" (to quote Herbert Marcuse's contradictory phrase), would work out happily. The evidence of history is to the contrary.

We have been told that a socialist state will remedy our social ills, but many thoughtful liberals draw back from the prospect of state socialism. It may be better, they say, to have a batch of capitalist speculators than a horde of bureaucrats. They do not want to hand society over to the speculators, but they do not find the bureaucrats attractive either. The unification of military, political, and economic power within the state can produce an engine of terrible force, and a managerial class can use this engine for its own power and aggrandizement. Socialism is a mask for tyranny unless accomplished by the democratization and decentralization of power. Rather than choose between big-business capitalism and socialist collectivism, we should encourage experiment in many different directions and cling to those innovations that prove themselves in practice.

The method of social experiment is in the best American democratic tradition. We should not only cherish this tradition but broaden and deepen it. We must strenuously insist upon the immunities and privacies guaranteed in the American Constitution, such as the rights of free speech, free assembly, freedom of religious belief, fair trial, and due process. It is difficult to exaggerate the importance of these rights. But we must also insist upon the broad social and civil rights implicit in our Constitution and spelled out in the United Nations Declaration of Human Rights. These include the right to equality before the law, the right to freedom from discrimination, the right to a decent livelihood, the right to adequate health care, the right to a good education, the right to share in the culture and progress of civilization, the right to beauty in our homes and cities and countryside, and, most inclusive of all, the right to realize our full potential as human beings. What we need is a bold agenda of reform and reconstruction—radical in its perception of the need for thoroughgoing changes, liberal in its attachment to intelligence and experimental method—which will realize, as nearly as possible, this full gamut of human rights.

The United States Supreme Court in recent years has interpreted our constitutional rights in a broad manner, finding in the Welfare Clause, the Civil War amendments, and other parts of the Constitution the rights implicit in Jefferson's phrase, "the pursuit of happiness." For example, in a case involving the condemnation of slum property for a redevelopment project, the court said: "Miserable and disreputable housing conditions may do more than spread disease and crime and immorality. They may also suffocate the spirit by reducing the people who live there to the status of cattle. They may indeed make living an almost insufferable burden. They may also be an ugly sore, a blight on the community which robs it of charm, which makes it a place from which men turn. The misery of housing may despoil a community as an open sewer may ruin a river. . . . The concept of the public welfare is broad and inclusive. . . . The values which it represents are spiritual as well as physical, aesthetic as well as monetary. It is within the power of the legislature to determine that the community shall be beautiful as well as healthy, spacious as well as clean, well-balanced as well as carefully patrolled." We have within our Constitution thus construed the basic ideals to guide us, and we have all the resources that we require—natural, technological, and human. We lack only the vision and the will to implement our ideals. In the idealism of our students I see evidence that these will be forthcoming.

The proper response to pressures from both the extreme left and the extreme right is to cling the more tenaciously to the Bill of Rights. It is to recall the great truths in the masterpieces of liberal thought, such as Milton's *Areopagitica* and Mill's *On Liberty*, while boldly scouting for new truths and insights. It is to recognize the difference between tested and critical beliefs, on the one hand, and popular emotional beliefs, on the other. It is to reject the sterile dogmas of the street, and to resist rather than yield to unwise community pressures. It is to preserve the toughness, the intransigence, and the spiritual vitality that give edge to democracy. It is to refuse to cower before wealth and armed might, and to admire compassion more than brute force. It is to appreciate the perennial wisdom in the words of Roger Williams: "None shall see the truth but the soul that loves it, and digs for it as for treasures of gold and silver, and is impartial, patient, and pitiful to the opposers."

Afterword

by Leonard W. Schroeter

I believe that that community is already in process of
dissolution, where each man begins to eye his neighbor
as a possible enemy, where non conformity with the
accepted creed, political as well as religious, is a mark
of disaffection; where denunciation, without specification
or backing, takes the place of evidence; where orthodoxy
chokes freedom of dissent; where faith in the eventual
supremacy of reason has become so timid that we dare not
enter our convictions in the open lists to win or lose.
—Judge Learned Hand

FIFTY YEARS AGO the state of Washington suffered from a
corrosive blight that spread into a grave national disorder,
commonly called McCarthyism.

On March 8, 1947, the Washington State legislature
passed House Concurrent Resolution No. 10, establishing
the Joint Legislative Fact-Finding Committee on Un-American Activities. The Resolution was introduced by a new
member of the legislature, Albert F. Canwell, who was appointed chairman of what became known as the Canwell
Committee. The Resolution read:

WHEREAS, these are times of public danger; subversive persons and groups are endangering our domestic unity, so as to leave us unprepared to meet aggression, and under cover of the protection afforded by the Bill of Rights these persons and groups seek to destroy our liberties and our freedom by force, threats, and sabotage, and to subject us to the domination of foreign power; and

WHEREAS, recent announcements by responsible officers of the federal government indicate the seriousness of the problem. J. Edgar Hoover, Director of the FBI, recently said:

> During the past five years, American Communists have made their deepest inroads upon our national life. Their propaganda, skillfully designed and adroitly executed, has been projected into practically every phase of our national life. The Communist influence has projected itself into newspapers, books, radios and the screen, some churches, schools, colleges, and even fraternal orders have been penetrated. . . .

WHEREAS, State legislation to meet the problem and to assist law enforcement officers can best be based on a thorough and impartial investigation by a competent and active legislative committee . . . [which] shall investigate the activities of groups and organizations whose membership include persons who are Communists, or any other organization known or suspected to be dominated or controlled by a foreign power, which activities affect the conduct of this state, the functioning of any state agency, unemployment relief and other forms of public assistance, educational institutions of this state supported in whole or in part by state funds, or any political program.

Canwell, elected from Spokane in the 1946 Republican landslide, had been an itinerant worker, a deputy sheriff, a printer, and an occasional newspaper employee. His committee convened its first hearings in January 1948, taking testimony concerning the operation of the Washington Pension Union. Almost fifty witnesses were called. Most were ex-Communists, many paid informers and professional witnesses who regularly provided their services to the House Un-American Affairs Committee (HUAC), the FBI, the Immigration and Naturalization Service (INS), and other government agencies whose principal activities were to ferret out the Communist conspiracy. On July 19, 1948, the Committee convened its second round of hearings with testimony focused on "subversive activities at the University of Washington." These hearings were widely publicized and socially disruptive.

In his formal report of the first hearings, Canwell concluded that "the overwhelming testimony [proved] the operation of a Communist bloc in our legislative sessions under the pseudonym of an established major political party." The public was warned that

(1) Communists in the State of Washington operate under, and undeviatingly follow, policies laid down for them by the Soviet government. (2) These policies are promulgated on a nationwide basis, and the activities of Communists in the State of Washington are coordinated with Communist activities in the other states of the union. (3) The dovetailed nationwide program is designed to create distrust of our form of government in the minds and hearts of the American people; create unrest and civil strife, and impede the normal process of State and National Government, all to the end of weakening and ultimately destroying the United States as a constitutional republic and thereby facilitating the avowed Soviet

[213]

purpose of substituting here a totalitarian dictatorship. Fantastic as this may appear to the uninitiated and the naive, the testimony produced at the public hearings clearly brings into view the extreme danger of the Soviet-directed Communist conspiracy to the peace and security of the people of the State of Washington and the United States. (*First Report, Un-American Activities in Washington State,* p. iv.)

Despite these frightening warnings, and the implication that the public needed the protections he could offer, Canwell failed to be elected for the legislative Senate seat in November 1948. The Canwell Committee completed its reports and moved its committee records to Olympia, Washington. Canwell never again held public office, losing a campaign for the Republican nomination to the U.S. Senate in 1950, suffering defeat for the seat of Congressman-at-Large in 1952, and failing to secure the Republican nomination for that seat in 1954.

After half a century, why should we reexamine the short, tawdry life of the Canwell Committee? Certainly Canwell himself, repudiated by the voters and no more than a footnote in the state's history (except to those who lived through the terror he instigated), could be left in obscurity. But yet, fifty years later, this chapter of social pathology demands revisiting and reexamining, if for no other reason than to reevaluate our own values in a different time. Milan Kundera observed, "The struggle of man against power is the struggle of memory against forgetting."

The University of Washington Press reissues Melvin Rader's classic account of his confrontation with the Canwell Committee, and its aftermaths, as part of a University-wide revisit to the Canwell past. The book was first published to national acclaim in 1969, more than twenty years after Rader had been targeted by the Committee. At that time Malcolm Cowley wrote, "His book is a disturbing yet also heartening chapter from recent American history." Cowley described it as "the story of a liberal wrongly accused during the McCarthy era, one of hundreds and thousands, but one with more courage and perseverance than others." And Edwin O. Guthman, the *Seattle Times* reporter, whose intensive investigation of Canwell's charges against Rader won for him the 1949 Pulitzer Prize, stated:

> We would like to think that what happened to Professor Melvin Rader could not happen in the United States, but it did. His story—his courage and forbearance, and his ultimate vindication—provides poignant insight into the overzealous pursuits of Communist sympathizers that raged after World War II.

But no kudos speak for the book or for Rader as well as he does for himself. The Preface to the first edition and its powerful Epilogue remain as compelling today as when they were written. The book has become a classic, in large part because its message and significance are timeless.

I do not need to reiterate the importance of the book or its ideas. My task has two parts. I can assist in calling attention to the continuing relevance of Rader's ideas and to their current applications. I also hope to give further emphasis to the dramatic dichotomy between the values of a progressive, rational humanist and the Canwell-type bully boy peddlers of current demonologies.

To explain the present relevance of our memory of the past, we must go back half a century. Those who lived through those times recall the chronic despair and hopelessness of the Great Depression, the frightening barbarity of ascendant fascism, the bloody aggressions and rapaciousness destroying peace and leading to World War II. We

[215]

looked down a long dark tunnel and saw no light at the end. Our very survival and the survival of democracy seemed at stake. Because of the war's horrible human toll, our awareness of the genocidal monstrosities of the Holocaust, and the awesome terror of the A-bomb, we had little time to savor the hopes of a brave new world, the creation of the United Nations, and the Universal Declaration of Human Rights—with their promises of generations of peace—when the Cold War commenced. But it was not only the Cold War, with a seemingly aggressive and dangerous new foe—the Soviet Union, but a cold war at home, a war that lent itself to hysteria, fear, and suspicion, to conformity, orthodoxy, and political repression. Once again we looked down the dark tunnel and could see no light.

There is a substantial literature describing Cold War repression and hysteria, yet it is difficult to recapture the mood of desperation and the sense of irrationality of those days. I have appended to this Afterword a list of readings that describe Washington State's manifestation of the hysteria. The McCarthy era gave its name to a form of political lawlessness characterized by the reckless destruction of individual rights and human lives, by vulgar demagoguery and overt reliance on exaggerated falsehoods. Its synonyms are still witch hunt and Inquisition, apt historic references to out-of-control abuse of power. The special tool of McCarthyism was the fear instilled in those named as heretics. Its model was HUAC, created in 1938, and chaired until the end of the war by Martin Dies, who had the prerogative of determining who was un-American.

HUAC had been exposing Communists for years before it was aped by Canwell and McCarthy. HUAC visited Seattle and the Pacific Northwest on numerous occasions, following up Canwell Committee hearings. Its traveling staff and members took testimony in Seattle in October 1952; March, May, June 1954; and again in March and June 1955. For the media, these were field days. For the victims, they brought fear. For the Committee, they were the same old carnival. For the American Civil Liberties Union and other public interest organizations, as well as for the attorneys who were dragooned into service, they represented continuing political repression. There was still no light at the end of the tunnel.

The Canwell Committee placed Washington among the first of the states to adopt devices to investigate so-called subversive activities. Before World War II, many states had criminal syndicalism acts, Red Flag laws, and general criminal statutes dealing with treason, rebellion, insurrection, and riots. These arose from a zeal to suppress the growth of the labor movement; the red scare of 1873-78; the communist-anarchist-labor scares of the late 1880s and the early 1890s, and of the first decade of the twentieth century; the effort to repress anti–World War I movements, and the red scares of 1919-20 and the late 1930s. Interestingly, historians evaluating these legislative efforts at subversion control appear not to have found a cause-and-effect relationship, either of social necessity or benefit. Without any apparent exception, such laws arose from political opportunity. The best survey of this phenomenon can be found in *The States and Subversion,* edited by Walter Gellhorn.

In 1940, California passed an anti-Communist subversion law, named after its author, Jack B. Tenney. In Illinois, there was a pre–World War II anti-subversive committee created by the Illinois legislature, and ignited by the public charges of Charles Walgreen, owner of a leading retail drug chain, that his niece had been indoctrinated with Communist ideologies by certain members of the University of Chicago faculty. An investigation ensued, with no result, but the committee structure remained, to be replaced in August 1947 by the Broyles Commission, officially designated the Seditious Activities Investigation Commission. Both in its

[217]

activities and its conduct, the Broyles Commission was similar to Washington's Canwell Committee.

The most important and authoritative book on state subversive activities is *Un-American Activities in the State of Washington: The Work of the Canwell Committee,* by Verne Countryman. At the time of writing, Professor Countryman was on the Yale Law School faculty. He subsequently was a distinguished faculty member of the Harvard Law School. An important chapter of his book was "the case of Melvin Rader." It was that case, more than any other factor, that led to the early demise of the Canwell Committee and to Canwell's retirement in disgrace from the political scene.

Judge Learned Hand's observations cited in the epigraph (p. 211) highlight one of the most socially disturbing phenomena in the culture of anti-communism—that the credibility and reliability of one's intellect, logic, and wisdom can be determined solely by one's political position. Suspicious hallmarks of belief and behavior included civil rights militancy, trade union advocacy, civil liberty commitment, feminism, and unorthodox sexual preferences.

Thus, the entire character of the period strongly constricted the range of views that could be expressed. There was little understanding or interest in individual variability, let alone tolerance for situational responses or human growth. Only conversion could buy salvation. And it could only be signified by naming names and bearing witness against one's former friends and colleagues.

Hangovers from these socially vicious litmus tests have persisted. Lawyers have some experience in assessing the credibility of witnesses, recognizing that the prejudices or self-interests of the witness may qualify the testimony no matter how logical and learned it appears to be. In determining what is true, or likely true, in a controversy over what factually occurred, one must, among other things, look at the credibility of the witnesses—their memories, perceptions, motives, and competence.

Although I do not feel neutral in terms of my preference between the protagonists in the Rader case, and I do not believe that the legal or historical circumstances were at all ambiguous, my training as a lawyer causes me to approach fact-finding in a particular and familiar way. In preparing this Afterword, it seemed to me essential to understand not only the historic context and the activities of the Canwell Committee, but the personalities, motivations, and credibility of State Representative Albert F. Canwell and University of Washington philosophy professor Melvin M. Rader.

I should state that I knew and liked Melvin Rader. We served together on the Board of Directors of the Washington Affiliate of the American Civil Liberties Union (ACLUW) for at least twenty years. I succeeded him as president of the ACLUW in 1963-64, and was president at the time of the John Goldmark libel trial,* actively participating in the plaintiff's case. I was also a member of the National ACLU Board, involved in the defense of the ACLU from the persistent attacks upon it by Canwell.

Rader was just three years older than Canwell, and both grew up in Eastern Washington. But there the similarity ended. Rader was a humanist, powerfully committed to the values of scholarship and the intellectual life, the search for truth, and the rule of law. He had a passion for a free and open society.

---

*I was also president when the United States Supreme Court declared unconstitutional Washington State's loyalty oath laws in a case brought by the ACLUW. The case, entitled *Baggett, et al. v. Odegaard,* included as one of its plaintiffs, Melvin Rader. I was involved in the structuring and planning of the case and assisted in representing the sixty-four University of Washington faculty members who joined

All the written evidence suggests that Canwell had contempt for intellectuals, scholarly pursuits, humanists, the search for truth, and the rule of law. To me, then and now, the good guy–bad guy dichotomy is clear. But the concrete, factual pivot of this drama was the accusation made by Canwell that Professor Rader was a member of the Communist party and had attended a Communist school for hard-core leadership at an upstate New York farm in the summer of 1938, a charge Rader flatly denied and successfully disproved. The sole witness against Rader was a black ex-Communist, George Hewitt, who was also a professional informer.

It is relevant that George Hewitt was employed in New York City by Generalissimo Chiang Kai-Shek's Washington, D.C., lobbyist, the China trading merchant Alfred Kohlberg. Kohlberg, in addition to his Chinese textile importing business, was publisher of the ultraconservative magazine, *Plain Talk,* and national chairman of the American Jewish League Against Communism. He subsequently received publicity as one of the principal sources of Senator McCarthy's allegations against members of the State Department, and was a member of a special committee formed by the Joint Committee against Communism in New York to cleanse the radio and television industry of pro-Communist actors, writers, producers, and directors. George Hewitt had numerous times denounced accused subversives for the INS and for HUAC, and had testified before the federal grand jury considering Whittaker Chambers's charges against Alger Hiss.

---

in the Constitutional challenge. As a private attorney, I had represented numbers of the plaintiffs in other contexts, some associated with civil liberties concerns. It is not coincidental that I would know many of those discussed in Rader's book, since I have practiced law in Seattle for forty-five years. I am a child of the Depression; witness to the rise of fascism; a veteran of World War II; and a member of ACLU for more than fifty years.

Hewitt returned to New York immediately after his closed testimony against Rader. He was never made available for cross-examination or any questioning under oath by authorities. At the time he disappeared, King County Prosecutor Lloyd Shorett was considering a perjury charge against him, filed by Rader. Telephone conversations with Hewitt strengthened Shorett's belief that Hewitt had lied. Kohlberg, in an effort to protect Hewitt, complained to U.S. Attorney General Tom Clark that Communists were harassing Hewitt, and that this would impair vital government functions, particularly those of the INS.

Ultimately, despite the complete unavailability of Hewitt, University of Washington President Raymond D. Allen and Washington State Attorney General Smith Troy determined from their investigations and hearings, that (1) Rader had been truthful; (2) Hewitt had lied; and (3) the Canwell Committee had no evidence that Rader had attended a Communist school or was at any time a member of the Communist Party. Charles Carroll, who succeeded Lloyd Shorett as prosecuting attorney, also made his own independent investigation and attempted to extradite Hewitt to Washington, without success. But the facts appeared clear. Rader's credibility was fully confirmed. Hewitt had become aphasic, and in 1950 he died, labeled a "false witness," despite the efforts of Kohlberg, Canwell, and the anti-Communist cabal to rehabilitate his reputation.

The preponderance of evidence had been as well established as it could be without the full processes of the law being applied as in a trial. But, in late 1963, an Okanogan jury considering the John Goldmark libel trial* had an opportunity to determine the truth of Canwell's claim that Rader had been a member of the Communist party. This

*John Goldmark, the plaintiff in this historic suit against Canwell, was my law partner and close friend from 1968 until his death.

time, another ex-Communist, professional witness, Barbara Hartle, testifying in Canwell's defense, stated that she knew Goldmark and fellow Communist Melvin Rader "to be under Communist Party discipline." On cross-examination, Hartle admitted that, although she had earlier named hundreds of Washington State people whom she claimed to be Party members, on all previous occasions when she had been asked about such matters, she had not included Rader in her testimony. Ed Guthman then testified that he had interviewed Hartle at an earlier time. When he had asked her if Rader was a member of the Communist party, she had denied that that was the case. The jury's verdict in favor of Goldmark presumably should have closed this question for eternity.

But there are other methods than litigation by which the search for truth can be continued. Among them is academic research, often strengthened by the judgments of history, after passions have cooled. The time frames within which protagonists acted may be helpful in the search for truth.

In 1939, Rader had written a book titled *No Compromise: The Conflict Between Two Worlds,* opening with Mussolini's dictum: "The struggle between two worlds [Democracy and Fascism] can permit no compromise." The book painstakingly analyzes Fascist doctrine within philosophical principles. In his introductory remarks, Rader states his thesis:

> Today the issue is not between this or that school of philosophy, but the possibility of the survival of any philosophy at all. The foundations of culture are tottering. Everything depends upon repairing the material and spiritual bases of life. Under these circumstances, philosophy dare not abstract itself from the political and economic struggles of the present day. No struggle is more crucial than that between Democracy and Fascism.

Rader saw Fascist doctrine and its practical embodiment as a flight from reason, and contended that lying journalism undermines public rationality and that Fascist irrationalism was an assault upon the very basis of democracy: "The foundations of our social order are tottering."

In 1939, Rader was an ardent proponent of what was then called the United Front against Fascism. Popular front ideology seemed imperative because of the broad range of views between liberal democrats and communists. But by 1969, in *False Witness,* Rader states:

> In retrospect, I still think that the ideal of the United Front was absolutely sound. If it had succeeded, it would have saved the world from incalculable misery, but it was betrayed by the appeasers and the Communists alike. The pact between Hitler and Stalin in the summer of 1939 was the culmination of treachery that had been present from the beginning.
>
> I do not deny that I made mistakes during the period of the United Front. It was some time before I realized that the Party joined united fronts in order to turn them into *Communist* fronts—that often it worked clandestinely, operating through secret members, to seize control from within . . . I was slow in realizing these facts. Too intense in my political commitments to see things with cold objectivity, I had not learned to look at myself or the world around me with humor or detachment. I saw the evils of depression and war very clearly, but I did not so clearly perceive the difficulties involved in creating a brave new world. (p. 39)

This belated apologia was in no way extraordinary. Subsequent criticisms of Rader's pre–World War II "softness" on Soviet communism could easily have been applied to millions of progressive democrats in most western societies, whose anti-Fascist ardor directed them to alliances with all anti-Fascist groups. *No Compromise* was written before the Nazi-Soviet pact and the Soviet invasion of Finland.

From September 1939 to December 1941, there was a reality basis for attitudinal changes, just as Pearl Harbor once again made the Soviet Union a desirable ally. By the end of World War II, the horrible revelations of the Holocaust and the passionate hopes for a brave new world impeded the rush to a cold war. But realities about Soviet foreign policy ambitions, in what now appeared to be a two-power world, need not rationally or realistically have led to the anti-Communist Cold War hysteria on the home front. It was clear then, as it is historically clear now, that the United States Communist party was small, sectarian, and powerless. The Soviet Union was a powerful, ruthless, totalitarian society. American Communist party members in large part followed a Soviet party line that was a myth and as deceptive as the line of the Communist hunters. Rader understood that and articulated it well at the Canwell hearings and later when he wrote *False Witness*. His political growth and understanding was a response to the passion of his times. His perceptions of reality had altered as that reality unfolded.

Melvin Rader's views on important public issues over a period of more than forty years were well documented and easily retrievable. Between the publication of *No Compromise* in 1939 and the 1979 edition of *False Witness*, the world had changed, and so had Rader. His fundamental values and personality, as reflected in his writings and his public life, remained relatively constant. But just as his political views and understandings had altered through time, his personal introspection and reflectiveness had helped him to mellow earlier passions.

When he died in June of 1981, at the age of seventy-seven,

his widow, Virginia, reflected, "We always felt that the Canwell business was not a major part of his life, although it was the most sensational. What really counted was his writing, his teaching, his efforts on behalf of the American Civil Liberties Union and prison reform." An editorial in the *Seattle Post-Intelligencer* was headlined, "Dr. Melvin Rader: A True Witness." He was described as

> a humanist, a gentle, thoughtful, unassuming man. Dr. Rader also was a courageous man. . . . The professor possessed a fierce independence and inner toughness that would not admit defeat. . . . For the rest of his life he defended civil liberties and the rights of the individual even though there always were ignorant people and sometimes vicious people who linked his name with Communism.

The editorial closes by praising his book and stating that the advice he gave to young people in *False Witness* is a fitting memorial,

> [T]o the young I say: "Keep right the arrows of the human spirit, but make sure that they are arrows of love and not hate. Of Eros, and not Thanatos."

Albert Canwell, now past ninety, has written no book, authored no reflective contemplations. But he has been in the public eye for half a century and has been frequently quoted. The transcripts of the hearings he chaired are informative about his views, his attitudes, and his thoughts on law and due process. He has been quoted as stating in 1946, when he was a candidate for the state legislature, that "if someone insists there is discrimination against Negroes in this country, or that there is inequality of wealth, there is every reason to believe that person is a Communist."

This type of thinking occurs throughout *Albert F. Canwell: An Oral History,* published in 1997 by the Washington State Oral History Program, Office of the Secretary of State.

In this 429-page document of interviews with Canwell, which he later edited, such strange disconnections abound: "the Party controlled the ACLU which was, in effect, the Communist apparatus . . .," "the disinformation level, they took over and he [Rader] became very reluctant and even wrote a book that got rave notices, unjustifiably. . . ." "Melvin Rader was a member of the Communist Party . . . one of their leading lights and longest members. . . ." "He was first recruited to the Communist Party on the campus of the University of Washington, recruited by a Soviet agent, a Communist agent, Lillian Reiseroff, who was brought here from Massachusetts to penetrate and organize the University of Washington. . . ." "In the Rader case, as in the Hiss case, we never came up with a membership card. . . ." "Their people the Party wished to bring [Rader] along to greater things, so it was not surprising to me that we didn't come up with that evidence." Canwell described Rader as "a weak person," "a good prospect to defect."

Although Canwell claimed that Rader was recruited into the Party in the early twenties, he never pursued finding Reiseroff to get her to testify before the committee. "It was one of the many leads that I didn't have time or the facilities to go into. . . . Rader himself was of no great importance. It was only the endeavors of the ACLU and others who made an issue of this." Canwell explains that the issue was made by Ed Guthman and Verne Countryman, who "were assigned to make an issue of it"—inferring that they, too, "were under Communist discipline."

Canwell repeatedly claimed that the FBI had informants who stated Rader was in the Communist party, but he "wouldn't embarrass the Bureau or destroy the confidential relationship that I had with various agents" by naming them. Canwell claimed that Rader always did the bidding of the Party and was useful to them. He added, "I've seen the same thing happen in the case of Ben Kizer, a very important Communist, who came to the place where he was senile and not dependable for party activity, but his name was extremely useful, and they even use it today. That was the way with Melvin Rader." Ben Kizer was a distinguished Spokane attorney and a prominent and respected national figure in the American Bar. His apparent sin was that he was a longtime member of the ACLU. Such reckless accusations have remained a characteristic of Canwell for more than half a century.

Canwell's bête noire was the ACLU, which he saw as Communist connective tissue for all of his foes. He claimed that the ACLU was "founded as a front for the international Communist Party centered in Germany prior to World War I." "They mount and maintain libel suits against active patriots (The Goldmark v. Canwell libel action was such an ACLU venture)," he told his interviewer, adding, "One hundred percent of the Goldmark [libel] case against Canwell was mounted by members of the ACLU." "ACLU contacts were responsible for arranging the torching of the Canwell Building containing the most extensive files and proofs of the perfidy of the ACLU and its agents." "Prime movers in the ACLU from the beginning have included such plotters as Felix Frankfurter, who trained and conditioned spies and traitors such as Alger Hiss." "One of the prize prospects developed by Frankfurter at Harvard was John Goldmark, a nephew of Louis Brandeis, Justice of the Supreme Court. . . ." "A sharp look needs to be taken at Louis Brandeis, John Goldmark, Felix Frankfurter, and their associates, many of whose antecedents had roots in the secret societies and political intrigues and subversion of the Hapsburg Empire in Austria, and in the case of Goldmark, in the political assassination of the defense minister of Austria."

Although Canwell insisted he was not anti-Semitic, his words are revealing of more complex feelings,

> I remember a Jewish friend of mine who said, back at the time we were exposing a number of them in the Hollywood industry who were Jewish, "Is every Communist a Jew?" And I explained to him, "No, but wherever there is a Jew Communist, he's going to the top, and it's just the nature of the animal. So you would see a lot of them in organized labor and Communist labor."

His contempt for Justices Frankfurter and Brandeis was overt, since he saw them as leaders and founders of the Communist conspiracy. Justice William O. Douglas was also of interest to him. "He was like Kizer. He was our boy and our responsibility to that degree." "Douglas had been involved in Yakima in some morals offense. He was always in the far liberal left camp." "It became a part of our knowledge that he was on the payroll of some of the criminal operations in the country." "Of course, there was Lewis Schwellenbach who became a federal judge here. He had been very active in the Communist apparatus in Seattle. The Communist party called him 'Lewie, the Laundry Man.' Eventually he became Secretary of Labor."

Canwell claimed to have personal knowledge that Judge Lloyd Shorett met with Morris Rappaport, the head of the Communist party in Washington State, in a rowboat in the middle of Elliott Bay, but he acknowledged, "I couldn't come into court and lay it on line. But it occurred. I had access to an enormous amount of electronic surveillance and agents who had worked at it."

> Judge Lloyd Shorett was close enough to this [Communist] operation that he'd have confidential meetings with Rappaport [Morris Rappaport]. Whenever he'd have an

interview, a meeting with Rap, they'd take a row boat and go out in Elliott Bay and have their discussions. So our agent was always very frustrated because he could never bug Prosecutor Shorett. Incidentally, Shorett was a key figure in the ACLU. . . . Ed Henry [later Judge Henry] who was Rader's attorney, ACLU. Everybody involved in that [Communist] apparatus was an ACLUer. Very interesting. Shorett was hand-in-glove with Ed Henry, Ed Guthman, and others in cooking up this phony Rader cause celebre.

In his oral history, he showed equal disrespect for law professors. Professor Verne Countryman was described as "a very tricky lawyer who was a functionary of the American Civil Liberties Union and served on its national committee." "He collaborated with one of the leading Communists in the writing of his book. It also was brought out by the government attorney, Tracy Griffin, that Verne Countryman had been recruited into the Communist Party on the campus of the University of Washington."

Father Francis Conklin, the Dean of the Law School at Gonzaga, had been a witness in the Goldmark libel case. He was condemned for being "an ACLU priest, and with the National Lawyers Guild, along with Ben Kizer, a Communist of world importance living in Spokane." ". . . The Soviet Department of Disinformation put the agents in place in America in the National Lawyers Guild and the ACLU."

The Dean of the University of Washington Law School in 1949 was Alfred Schweppe, a distinguished Seattle lawyer and, later, a leader of the Bar, who had opined that the Canwell Committee was unconstitutional. Canwell described him as "a dummy. He wasn't a Communist. He was just a fathead."

In reviewing Canwell's pungent opinions, the enormous

chasm between myth and reality is evident. The irrationality, disrespect for facts or fact-finding, distaste for the processes of the law, and lack of respect for human dignity present in his oral history, were his hallmarks as the Chair of the Joint Fact-Finding Committee on Un-American Activities. Judging from the oral history interviews, there is no reason to believe that his views have changed in fifty years. The Communist conspiracy is as real to him today as it was in 1947.

There was a conspiracy. But it was an official one, not one perpetrated by University of Washington professors, perceived as political heretics. The tragedy is that in 1947, the entire state was cowed by Canwell, just as the nation was held hostage by the J. Edgar Hoovers and Joseph McCarthys for so long a period of time that the mythology propagated by them became institutionalized.

If we look at the principal American heresy tribunals in the last half of the twentieth century, we note that it is not their longevity, or even their legitimacy, that is critical. It is the mood and mythology they created. All of them were politically conceived and executed, largely by Congress and state legislatures, although sometimes by executive order. HUAC, the longest lived, died before its thirtieth birthday, having been chaired by persons not only undistinguished but notable for their mediocrity. Martin Dies, J. Parnell Thomas, John S. Wood, Harold Velde, Francis Walter are now gratefully forgotten. The Loyalty Boards established under Truman's Loyalty Order of 1947 either expired out of desuetude or were stricken by the courts as unconstitutional. The Internal Security Subcommittee of the Senate Judiciary (SISS) preceded and outlived the McCarthy Committee, but its chairs, Pat McCarran, William Jenner, and James Eastland, were merely wens on our political face, even at that time. The Subversive Activities Control Board created by Congress as a consequence of the McCarran

Internal Security Act of 1950 had a short and troubled life and was vigorously exposed by a senator from the state of Washington, Harry P. Cain, a conservative Republican, who still believed that the Bill of Rights was relevant. Senator McCarthy's "permanent" subcommittee on Investigation of the Senate Committee on Government Operations was shunted out of existence after several years because of the unlawful, public misbehavior it had perpetrated during McCarthy's frightening sway. And, the Canwell Committee would have been a sordid blip in the state's history's but for the fear it created and the legacy of distrust that it left us.

The FBI under J. Edgar Hoover was a far more powerful and dangerous instrument of political repression. In his fifty-year leadership of the agency, Hoover contributed heavily to a system of cultural myths that importantly influenced American life and politics: the chauvinist myth of "Americanism" as a divinely ordained political ideology and way of life; the concept of domestic "national security" that must always prevail over the right to dissent; the conviction that the nation was under permanent threat of internal subversion by sinister, godless Communists who would stop at nothing to gain their ends.

Central to Hoover's role was his cultivation and exploitation of the anti-Communist mania. We need not measure his failures in dealing with organized crime, and its professionalization. We need not remind ourselves that corporate crime, a far greater producer of deaths, injuries, and multibillion dollar theft, never was given his attention. Hoover used his prestige as the nation's number one anti-subversive champion to immunize himself from criticisms for his failure as head of the nation's criminal investigation bureau.

The reception given Hoover's pronouncements by congressmen, the news media, and some public figures was an adulation rarely seen in democratic societies, although commonplace in totalitarian regimes. Hoover was a genius of sorts in the public relations promotion of his own image. Patriotic, incorruptible, super-vigilant, and endowed with old-time American values, as he painted himself, he exercised unchecked control over the mechanisms of political intelligence, which led to the institutional transformation of the FBI into an autonomous and self-perpetuating political police force that made a mockery of our democratic process.

Hoover, like McCarthy, like Canwell, like Martin Dies, can find few supporters in these times. But the legacy left by these men can still silence dissidents and permit the reign of irrationality and social delusion.

Rader triumphed over his ordeals because he was able and willing to fight back. He elicited support from the media, from public officials, from his own lawyers, university colleagues, and, most of all, from the still powerful tradition in the Pacific Northwest that nurtured a strong ACLU and public interest community. In an ultimate sense, however, it was Rader's own strong faith in the democratic process, his powerful commitment to the values of an open society and civil liberties. He took on Canwell and Hewitt, not only because it was the right thing to do but because discrediting the committee and its star witness was an opportunity to vindicate his own reputation and perhaps to end the witch hunt that was decimating the University and the community. He was the right symbol at the right time, and with a little luck, he succeeded. His was a rare success story followed by the admonition that fifty years later, the same battles need to be fought. Only the names and themes are different. Today, each of us might be able to identify our least favorite mythology and categorize it as McCarthyism. But it could also be called Canwellism, or Hooverism, or, unfortunately, Americanism.

The ultimate lesson of the Canwell experience is that what Canwell clumsily represented has, by the end of this century, not disappeared. Those who have exercised, and continue to exercise, unrestrained power that undermines the defined authority of the constitutional system of checks and balances, are still a force to be reckoned with. Those who nurture lawlessness, justified by the expansive emergency doctrines of internal and national security, and the cult of subversive conspiracy at home and abroad, have in fact established a dominant ideology in the post-war American empire. Even the brief public dishonor of Nixon or the venal hubris of Newt Gingrich do not stand in the way of the toxins to a democratic environment. Though the demagogues of un-American investigations have come and gone, the cult of subversive conspiracy survives in the many legislative enactments it spawned and in the designs for covert operations it institutionalized. The FBI, national security agencies, IRS, State Department, INS, Department of Justice, grand juries, Bureau of Alcohol, Tobacco and Firearms, drug enforcement agencies, and special White House units continue to carry on surveillance of certain groups and individuals.

In the fifty years since the Canwell Committee, America's heretics have included civil rights and black nationalist organizations, women rights advocates, anti-war and peace movements, student agitators, environmental activists, and public interest groups seeking to limit and counter corporate power.

We need to understand the modern national security state as it controls dissent, engineers consent, and defines the boundaries of the free market in ideas. This is essential if there is to be any hope of people controlling their own destinies. Our customs and myths, our ways of seeing reality and believing fiction, alter and affect our public policies, laws, and institutions.

[233]

We need to understand that there will always be political struggle over a culture's collective memory. Those who define the past and manipulate its meaning will most certainly control and organize the future. The cult of subversive conspiracy disarmed liberals and at times neutralized even the ACLU, not to mention the decisions of judges. Conditioned by anti-communism, they accepted the Cold War institutional innovations and political compromises and made them permanent, essential components of the national security state.

Canwellism, like McCarthyism, was in effect a postwar program to demobilize the New Deal adherents of social justice, economic equality, democratic promise, and multilateral cooperation. It was designed to restore the power and predominance of the American Right and to disarm its opponents. Those in power define what is real. Anyone who questioned that definition must be part of the security problem.

A recent book, *Fire Wall: The Iran-Contra Conspiracy and Coverup* (New York: W.W. Norton, 1997), by Lawrence E. Walsh, documents a more recent American example of the misuse of power, both domestic and international. Judge Walsh, the Iran-Contra independent counsel, a lifelong conservative Republican, who had served on the federal bench and who shared the foreign policy views of the Reagan Administration, writes of the secret scheme to finance the Contra war in Nicaragua against the elected Leftist Sandinista government by selling weapons to Iran. This scheme was in defiance of the law and circumvented the Constitution. The operation could be successful only through lies and coverups.

Nonetheless, there were facts that could be and were established. The independent counsel details his six-year-long battle to break through the firewall the White House officials built around President Reagan and Vice-President

Bush after the Iran-Contra scandal exploded in November 1986. At the top levels of the administration, it is apparent that everyone knew that Reagan had approved the shipments to Iran and that Attorney General Edwin Meese had lied to the public to cover up the fact. The secretary of state, the defense secretary, the director of the CIA, and a National Security Council (NSC) advisor all were involved.

Sometimes the lies and the mythmaking finally are revealed, even though many Americans still do not understand that presidents often lie, under the guise of national security or when the truth might undermine or threaten their power.

To give another example, it must be clear from recent disclosures concerning the tobacco industry that top executives of multibillion dollar companies do lie to prevent the limitation of their gigantic profits by regulation or exposés of health hazards. They assemble stables of false witnesses and inundate the popular media with attacks upon those who warn us of health risks. They attack the medical community and environmentalists as "special interests." And they seek to "reform," by destroying, our civil justice system to prevent plaintiffs' attorneys from using the historic tort system for its constitutional purpose—to make the powerful accountable for the harm they have done.

The lessons to be learned from the Canwell Committee must be relearned again and again. There is a fundamental difference between individual political, artistic, aesthetic, and scientific opinion and the fact-finding processes of courts and governments. Individual opinions, tastes, and aesthetics must be more than tolerated. They must be respected, because society's interest requires inquiry, challenge, non-conformity, and the exercise of creativity, intellect, and reason. If we wish to assure that justice is done in our courts, we operate under rules of law. Government power is constrained by constitutional principles such as due process of law, freedom of speech, academic freedom, and, most of all, by our certain knowledge that truth is elusive.

Orthodoxy and tyranny can survive only if they are enthroned and protected by immunities and the suppression of challenge. We revisit the painful period of the Canwell Committee and that era in American life we call McCarthyism, not as neutrals, but as witnesses to historical shame. We do so to apply the lessons we should have learned then to our contemporary problems, and to arm ourselves for the necessary continued protection of the social values found in an open democratic society.

Seattle, Washington
October 1997

Sources and Selected Further Readings

Albert F. Canwell: An Oral History. Washington State Oral History Program, Office of the Secretary of State, Olympia, 1997.

Andrews, Bert. *Washington Witch Hunt.* New York: Random House, 1948.

Barth, Alan. *The Loyalty of Free Men.* New York: Viking Press, 1951.

Belfrage, Cedric. *The American Inquisition, 1945-1960: A Profile of the "McCarthy Era."* New York: Thunder's Mouth Press, 1989 (originally published in 1973).

Caute, David. *The Great Fear: The Anticommunist Purge under Truman and Eisenhower.* New York: Simon and Schuster, 1978.

Countryman, Verne. *Un-American Activities in the State of Washington: The Work of the Canwell Committee.* Ithaca: Cornell University Press, 1951.

Davis, Elmer H. *But We Were Born Free.* Indianapolis: Bobbs-Merrill, 1954.

Dwyer, William J. *The Goldmark Case: An American Libel Trial.* Seattle and London: University of Washington Press, 1984.

First Report, Un-American Activities in Washington State. Report of the Joint Legislative Fact-Finding Committee on Un-American Activities. Washington State Legislature. Olympia, Washington, 1948.

Gellhorn, Walter. *The States and Subversion.* Ithaca, NY: Cornell University Press, 1952.

Gillmor, Daniel S. *Fear, the Accuser.* New York: Abelard-Schuman, 1954.

Griffith, Robert. *The Politics of Fear: Joseph McCarthy and the Senate.* Amherst: University of Massachusetts Press, 1987 (originally published in 1973).

Kahn, Gordon. *Hollywood on Trial.* New York: Boni and Gaer, 1948.

Navasky, Victor. *Naming Names.* New York: Viking Press, 1980.

Potter, Charles E. *Days of Shame.* New York: Coward-McCann, 1965.

Rader, Melvin. *No Compromise: The Conflict Between Two Worlds.* New York: Macmillan, 1939.

Sanders, Jane. *Cold War on Campus: Academic Freedom at the University of Washington.* Seattle and London: University of Washington Press, 1979.

Taylor, Telford. *Grand Inquest: The Story of Congressional Investigations.* New York: Simon and Schuster, 1955.

Trumbo, Dalton. *The Time of the Toad: A Study of Inquisition in America.* West Nyack, NY: Journeyman Press, 1982.

Wechsler, James A. *The Age of Suspicion.* New York: Random House, 1953.